"POT SHORTS is like the history of the Merry Pranksters told by *Prairie Home Companion*. Outlaws living a simple life on the land, new age warriors carving a life from the fertile land of Mendocino, families and communities threatened by helicopters, pirates, betrayal from the inside, and stupid social prejudices. This is what the counter culture was/is all about. And it's about the spirit that hopefully will come to sing to all of us, that life is caring for friends and family, and hanging together, and talking the talk and walking the walk. This is the story of a close-knit community that saw their path and walked it proudly. Studs Terkel would be proud; so would Ken Kesey."

– Steve Nicolaides, Producer of *Boyz N the Hood, School of Rock, Stand By Me*

As this merciless prohibition draws closer to an end, I can now offer you these stories.

Enjoy the read,
Joe Smith
10-1-15

pot shorts

Pot Shorts

Meet Lola and Luke, two of the original pot farmers who participated in the evolution of the northern California pot culture over the past 35 years. They lived among a community who shared the same secret lives and at times lived under the same blanket of fear and paranoia. Their shared experiences and difficulties created tight bonds and long lasting friendships that are evident throughout the book. These are short stories as told by the outlaws who lived in the heart of the notorious Emerald Triangle. Often provocative, sometimes thrilling and always told with the love and honesty that this unique community shares.

pot shorts

lola larkin
with zoey smith

straight from the mouths of the people who lived it!

Copyright © 2014 Lola Larkin, Alicia Berkeley Publishing. All rights reserved, including the right of reproduction or distribution, in whole or in part, in any form whatsoever, without written permission of the author or publisher.

Alicia Berkeley Publishing
P.O. Box 420, Healdsburg, CA 95448

Illustrations by: CJ

First Edition: January 2014
ISBN-13: 978-1493567812 [Paperback Edition]

Printed in the United States of America.

AUTHOR'S NOTES

This book is a nonfiction narrative of interviews and short stories. All of the stories are marijuana related, hence the title *Pot Shorts*. The characters and the names of places have been changed to protect the innocent.

— Lola Larkin

Dedicated to the people of the mountain who had the courage and spirit to live their lives in the way they believed.

Contents

Introduction xvii

1. **MOUNTAIN BOUND** 1
   - Luke And Lola 3
   - Toby And Midget 8
   - Gator And Goldie 10
   - Cassie 13
   - Lily 16
   - What Do You Do For A Living? 21
   - Driving To Dry 23
   - Jed 26
   - Cooper 29
   - Community Bonds 32

2. **FROM START TO *hopefully* FINISH** 35
   - The Basics 37
   - Difficulties Of Growing 39
   - Trim Crews 41
   - To Trim Or Not To Trim 44
   - Flee! 46
   - Selling The Product 48
   - Middlemen 50

Contents

3. CAMP 53
- The Unlawful Side Of Unlawful 55
- Citizens React 59
- Eagle Eye 63
- Human Nets 65
- Too Sad To Watch 67
- First Year 69
- Bad Roll Of The Dice 72
- It's A Bummer Please 73
- Cut And Run 76
- Infrared 78

4. RIP OFFS 81
- Booby Traps 83
- Ripped In The Boonies 89
- Guard Not 91
- Snipper 94
- Star Wars 95
- Home Invasion 97
- Not Very Neighborly 100
- Guardian Angels 102
- Nightmare With Mister Jones 104

5. BAD JUJU 115
- Bad Boys 117
- Tough Love 120
- Old Man And Wild Hungarian Woman 122
- Wigged Out 125

Contents

- Hog-Tied 128

6. **WILD LIFE** 131
   - Road Kill For Dinner 133
   - Wardens, Growers And Bears, Oh My! 134
   - It's Not Bambi Anymore 139

7. **IT'S A MIXED BAG** 141
   - Being In Town 143
   - Green Soup 147
   - Toyota Commercial 149
   - Incognito 151
   - Magoo 153
   - Bitten By The Bug 155
   - Hair Straight Up 156
   - Bean 157
   - Money Woes 160

8. **LIFE ON THE MOUNTAIN** 167
   - The Day Pack 169
   - Wanting Babies 173
   - Growing Up On The Mountain 175
   - Gathering Of The Hill Folk 183
   - Holidays 185

9. **LAST BUT NOT LEAST** 189
   - High Flyers' Club 191

Contents

- This Land Is Your Land, This Land Is My Land 194

Acknowledgments 197

INTRODUCTION

Lola is a tall, slender woman, with dark brown hair and a lovely olive complexion. Her very best feature is her generous heart. She has a positive energy, is welcoming to friends and strangers, is quick to laugh, and appreciates people with a good sense of humor.

I first met Lola while we were dancing at a party over a decade ago. Her passion for life filled the room and I liked her immediately. She talked to me about wanting to go to Burning Man, a unique festival in the Nevada desert. Plans began, we merged friends and families, and off we went. Our friendship was turbo-charged by that experience.

Lola began telling me stories of the mountainous area where she used to live and trusted me with the revelation that she was a pot farmer. I had never known a serious pot farmer before. She told me how her friends would get together at dinner parties to talk about "the old days on the mountain." She loved the stories and wanted to preserve the history of this unique community, with a hope to shed light on the diversity of people possibly enlightening those with a stereotypical view of pot farmers.

I was fascinated with the stories. She invited me to listen to tapes of those conversations and our collaboration on this book began.

POT SHORTS

Lola and Luke and their old friends, all had several things in common. Here is how Lola described them:

> *Everyone came to the hills in the late '70s to early '80s, looking to get away from the rat race and back to nature, leaving decent paying jobs behind. Most of us enjoyed smoking pot and started growing it for our own use before seeing it as a way to make ends meet financially. Though most of us were college-educated, we had no desire to return to our mainstream jobs.*
>
> *None of us had moral concerns about growing for profit, since we didn't buy into the government's prohibition stance regarding something we found not only enjoyable, but harmless.*
>
> *We were also at the age where we wanted children. We began having babies and raising families while becoming very close as a group; we held a common secret that we couldn't share with the outside world.*
>
> *The main differences between growing 35 years ago and growing today are the vast number of people doing it, the increased public awareness of its harmlessness, and greatly reduced pressure from law enforcement. Back in the day, you lived in fear and paranoia and only confided in your close friends and neighbors — those who were doing the same*

Introduction

thing. There was constant fear of getting either busted or ripped-off, and anxiety and gut aches were common. Nowadays rip-offs are less likely due to the sheer numbers of plants. There is safety in numbers.

Back then, there were no phones or internet to gather information on growing techniques, so trial and error was the only approach. We had to learn how to deal with insects, mice, gophers, rats, deer, bears, mold, rot, and in later years, spider mites and white powdery mildew. We grew in heavy shade to avoid detection, using only shovels and picks, and carrying everything on our backs, and we were proud to get one quarter-pound per plant.

The people I'm talking about are like family to me. I have known most of them for around 35 years and I know them well. We have shared joyful times and hard times. We have grown up together, raised our children together and grown pot together. Living in fear of getting caught, living outside the law, brought us closer together.

None of us felt like we were doing anything wrong, but we knew what we were doing was illegal. We could not talk about it to other people but we could trust and feel safe with each other. These good friends are some of the most honest, good-hearted, open-minded and generous people I have ever known.

Reminiscent of the days of Prohibition almost a century ago, this book reflects today's modern prohibition, our generation's culture and experience. I'm happy that these secret stories are seeing the light at last.

— Zoey Smith

mountain bound

POT SHORTS

LUKE AND LOLA

LOLA: The only thing Luke and I seemed to have in common when we met was our love of nature and a strong work ethic. We both loved the outdoors and liked to camp. I was a young hippie — free-spirited and, at that time, knee deep in drugs and health food. I was also a major animal lover and pacifist and wouldn't even kill a bug.

Luke, on the other hand, was an outdoorsman who loved his guns and enjoyed hunting and fishing. He was a daredevil, always living on the edge. As far as pets were concerned, Luke loved his dogs but indoor pets were not part of his upbringing — just the opposite of mine where our pets had the run of our home. Luke and I had to come to an agreement *fast* over that one.

Luke and I first met in college. He had long blond hair then, beautiful green twinkling eyes and a killer grin. He was and still is wiry and agile, a prankster who loves to think up silly outdoor games. Luke has a good sense of humor and always makes me laugh. He wasn't into getting high — such a refreshing change from hanging out with people who just wanted to get stoned.

Luke would take me out into the woods where we would go target shooting with his rifles, shotguns, and pistols. We often went camping and fishing up in the hills, or to the beach to dive for abalone. We would build a fire, cooking the abalone right in its shell with spices he brought. He was such a good diver that when I dove with him, I had my limit in no time.

Like most hunters, Luke is an avid animal lover and conservationist. Also a birdwatcher, he can tell you the species of a bird when it's no more than a speck in the air.

When I first went to a turkey shoot with his family, I learned where he got his skills. He, his dad and his brothers always won all the prizes. They were a whole family of crack shots.

I had never met anyone like Luke. He was fun-loving and playful, and I loved being around him. He told me that I was his biggest fan, and I'm proud to say it's still true.

When we started to dream of getting some land for ourselves, I believed he would be the perfect person to do it with.

We both worked at a hospital in the city, and on our days off we would drive around northern California in our VW bus, searching for land. In 1978 we finally found an old hunting cabin on 40 acres, one hour north of Ridgeville, that we could afford. It cost us $22,000 with $3,000 down. At the time, ground squirrels, wood rats and deer mice called it their home, and it probably should have been torn down. It was shelter, however, and we lived on a tight budget so we just started trying to fix the place up. We didn't have a generator or skill saw or other power tools, but we had a chain saw. That's what we used to build with.

Mountain Bound

We had a clawfoot bathtub and needed to run a pipe through the floor, but didn't have cordless drills back then. So Luke said, "Stand back," and he shot a hole through the floor with his shotgun. How else would one make a hole in the floor? It was crude carpentry, but the pipe fit perfectly.

I had purchased my first house in a small town in Sonoma County in 1976. Luke helped fix it up and then we sold it for a profit. Plus, we both made a good living working at the hospital, so we had some decent savings to live off for awhile. We didn't have jobs after leaving the hospital but figured we would move up to our property and work it out when we got there. We were so excited.

Luke was growing a few plants on our new property but we never planned on making an actual living doing it. When we first moved up I got a job, driving a couple of hours to town to work with developmentally challenged adults. Luke was working for a local retired couple, Toby and Midget, making $3.50 an hour digging ditches and doing hard labor. Toby always said Luke was the best worker he'd ever had. To hear Luke tell it, he was so anxious to get the work done for Toby that he toiled like a mad man so he could get back home and dig his own holes for his plants. There were no big pots in those days and we didn't have a rototiller, so he used a pick and shovel. It was a lot of hard work.

I was always gut-wrenchingly anxious about getting caught growing pot and I also hated lying to people when asked what kind of work we do. I spent a lot of time trying to make legal money without having to drive down the hill every day. I created some stained glass windows and sold a few. I also had a mail order business with a good friend on the hill.

I finally found that buying and selling property was something I was good at. I liked searching for inexpensive houses to fix up and rent or sell. Living on the mountain gave us the opportunity to discover land deals. Luke turned out to be good at developing springs and figuring out where to put in roads and ponds. Over the years, with these skills, we became property managers.

Because of the illegality of growing marijuana, it was hard to meet new people unless they lived on the hill and shared our lifestyle — and, of course, it's impossible to develop any close relationships when you can't be truthful.

Our friends from the city who knew we were growing sometimes said they thought we were lucky to live as we did. Yes, we loved our lifestyle but it wasn't just luck. The work was extremely difficult, and there is a high level of constant anxiety and fear that comes with being an "outlaw." It's a lifestyle that isn't suited to everyone.

We were fortunate to have the friendship and support of the neighbors we did, neighbors with whom we developed deep relationships and that we loved and trusted.

Mountain Bound

Simply put, you have to love the lifestyle on the hill to make it work.

TOBY AND MIDGET

Toby and Midget, a retired couple, were the very first people we met on the hill. Of our friends, they were the first to buy property up in that neck of the woods, back in 1969. They drove five hours each way from the city to their property almost every weekend for six years, bringing supplies to build the home that they eventually lived in. Toby had been a contractor specializing in demolition, and Midget was an ex-navy seaman, working as Toby's bookkeeper.

Toby is a big, strong, handsome man with a bit of a limp from a botched job of back surgery. He is an extremely hard worker, quite capable, with many skills.

Midget is a small woman, with short brown hair and great legs. She has a dry, witty sense of humor and is tough as nails. No one wants to cross Midget; if you get out of line, she can put you in your place in a heartbeat.

There is no point in bothering to whine either, because she won't get out the violin for you. I've _tried_ to complain to her sometimes, but she would just say sarcastically, "Oh, you kids have it so hard," using that tone, then giving me that look, while shaking her head with a chuckle.

Toby and Midget were both old school, no-nonsense Republicans with hearts of gold. They were always ready to help out the young hippie kids but first *each person had to earn their respect by proving themselves honest and hardworking.*

We are still very good friends so I guess we passed the test.

TOBY: Midget and I used to come up from the Bay Area and work on our house every weekend. Usually Saturday afternoons we'd take a drive in our old Scout. One day we stopped by the creek. I don't know if we were hunting or what, but we walked above the road and came across what we thought was a vegetable garden. We started looking a little closer, and wondered if maybe it was marijuana. This was the early '70s and we had never seen it before. There weren't many people up here back then, so we were surprised to see a garden with barefoot tracks all around it. A week later we went back to take another look … and it was completely gone.

Maybe they saw our tracks and got worried. That was the beginning of our curiosity.

POT SHORTS

GATOR AND GOLDIE

 Luke and I would take our motorcycles on this old skid trail running all the way up the side of the mountain. It wasn't our property, but in those days there were so many absentee property owners that we felt free to explore anywhere we wanted. One of our favorite places to ride was through one piece that actually had a sweet little picnic table out on a point in a meadow. It overlooked the whole canyon below.

 One day, while out on a ride, we spotted a young man and woman sitting at that picnic table, along with a little girl about two years old. We were just dismounting our bikes when that naked little two-year-old, with her red hair and freckled face and wearing just her tiny little cowboy boots, came straight over to us and announced, "I'm Shortcake. Who are you?"

 That was the first time we met Gator, Goldie, and Shortcake. It was their property.

 Gator is known for his big smile and big heart, not to mention his mutton chops. A finance manager for a government agency in Santa Barbara County, he had purchased his property in 1971 — 40 acres for $15,000. He used to come up hunting with a cousin. After we got to know him, there was always a cold beer waiting, letting us and other friends know they were welcome to drop by his house at any time.

Mountain Bound

Goldie was a building supervisor for Santa Barbara's sanitation district. She has blond hair and beautiful blue eyes that reflect her kind openness. You always know where you stand with Goldie.

They both worked full time and soon realized the babysitter was the one who experienced all of their baby's "firsts" and not them. This got Gator and Goldie to thinking, "Why does our babysitter know more about our child than we do?" They said it became obvious to them that they were working too much — this just wasn't the way they thought their life should be. So they chose to take three months off work, do something different, and spend time with their baby. Hopping in their travel trailer, they landed on their property, and began thinking about what the next step might be. Gator and Goldie decided, "This is cool. We could make it up here." Coincidentally, that was July 4, 1984. Independence Day.

GOLDIE: Probably within a few weeks of moving up here, Joker, our neighbor down the hill, came up with his head hanging and a sheepish "tail between his legs" attitude.

He told us, "My wife made me come up because the helicopters are flying and we're kinda worried about your safety. My wife said I have to tell you that I've got plants on your property and I'm using your pond. By the way, it's about to run out of water."

GATOR: I said, "Well, what can I do to help?"

POT SHORTS

I ended up helping Joker and he ended up giving us a quarter pound of weed at the end of the year.

The next year we decided to try putting some plants in ourselves but we had no clue about what to do. Eventually we put our first plants in, not far from where our house is today. Within a few weeks the wild turkeys came and just chewed the shit out of them.

That was our first growing experience.

CASSIE

I met Cassie when I was working at the hospital. I always thought she looked like Ingrid Bergman. With auburn hair and hazel eyes, she was strong and big boned. Always a hard worker, she worked day shift when I was on swing. I didn't get to really know her until she joined our softball team. She had an arm on her like a rocket and she ended up being our shortstop.

When I moved up to Ridgeville, Cassie would come to visit me. I lived 50 minutes up a dirt road and a four hour drive from her house, but she had no problem coming up. Very independent, she had no fear of anything. In those days with no phones, letting us know when you were coming wasn't possible, but she would take a chance and just come up and then camp out if we weren't there.

Cassie was a great gardener and loved her roses. Whenever she was here, you could tell how much she loved it. She is the type that is always there to help a friend, and always jumped in to help with any projects we were working on. And there were <u>lots</u> of projects.

GOLDIE: First time I ever saw Cassie, we were living on that little point there, with the travel trailer. And I saw Cassie driving by on a two-wheel motorcycle with a dog sitting on the gas tank. I thought, "I want to meet that girl."

POT SHORTS

That picture will remain vivid in my mind for the rest of my life.

TOBY: I remember the first time I saw you, Cassie. I had just met Luke and Lola a few weeks before and I stopped by to say, "Hello." There was Cassie, crawling into Luke and Lola's house through a window — and she was stuck — half in and half out.

She just looked at me and said, "Hi, I'm a friend of Luke and Lola."

CASSIE: (Laughing) Even though Luke and Lola weren't home, I had decided I was going to stay for a while. I didn't like to stay in their house without their permission so I was sleeping on the outside beds. I had brought some food, but most of what I brought needed to be cooked. So I would crawl through their kitchen window to use the stove for my meals. That was where Toby found me.

LOLA: We all used to sleep outside in nice weather. We would line up the beds on the ground and all our company would just sleep outside. I remember how much we loved watching shooting stars and satellites. The stars were just so vivid without the town lights around.

When it was raining and cold, we sometimes would all crowd around on our little bed inside, drive the car up to the window, and hook our battery up to a tiny little TV. We only got one channel but it was a pretty big deal at the time.

CASSIE: Every person that came up for a visit, I would take on Goldie and Gator's road, which would also drop down through Luke and Lola's property. That was always a fun place to take new people — and scare 'em to death on the slurry road. You know, before this road was in here when it was just a skid trail. Luke was just like a motocross rider. I was new to motorcycles, but Luke'd be flying all the way up there and flipping his bike.

I also remember a time we were in your kitchen, Lola. You were trimming pot at that old enamel yellow table. It was before you remodeled the cabin — in '78 or '79. And Luke said to me, "I'm going to teach you a new profession: trimming pot. I'm giving you free work experience, career training, *and* you'll get paid for it." I had no idea I would ever be doing this — ever. I had come up here to get away, basically to escape from my previous relationship, and Luke put me to work. I certainly didn't expect Luke's words to be so prophetic and to still be trimming 35 years later.

POT SHORTS

LILY

We first met Lily the same day we found our property. She lived halfway down the mountain, where the power poles ended at that time, which was 1978. As Luke and I were driving off the hill, we saw Lily outside her trailer, hanging laundry on her clothesline. We stopped to ask her a few questions about the area and, with her strawberry-blond hair and welcoming eyes, we immediately liked her. I recall her telling us that she lived on her parents' land, and they were the only ones on the mountain with a phone, which we were welcome to use anytime.

Her dialog was colorful — the way she drew an analogy between the present and some backwoods wisdom she seemed to have. Sometimes people did not quite understand what she was talking about, but they usually got the gist.

Very spiritual and talented, she was a pleasure to listen to and never failed to make me laugh.

At one point, Lily and I started a mail order business together, becoming lifelong friends in the process. Once, when we needed to go to the city for a trade fair, I discovered that she had never spent the night away from her husband, Sonny. She got through that night just fine and good-naturedly endured my teasing.

Lily is a true hippie and a very intelligent country bumpkin.

Mountain Bound

LILY: Sonny and I came here in 1976 with no plans whatsoever to grow pot. My parents had bought the land and Sonny and I lived in a tipi while selling Native American jewelry. I had developed a trade route in New Mexico and we traveled around as wholesalers, selling our jewelry. We also learned how to make moccasins and had our own cottage industry for a long while before it dawned on us to grow weed.

The idea came to us when we outfitted an entire family with very expensive custom footwear through a shop in Eureka. Because they looked like two cents waiting on change, Sonny took the guy aside and asked, "How are you paying for this?"

The guy said, "Well, I grow marijuana."

Right then the proverbial light bulb went off and we asked, "Okay, how many acres do you have?"

We then bought a little trailer, put it on my parents' land and started growing weed the summer of 1975. We didn't know squat and made every mistake you could possibly make.

Stone cold rookies, we ended up putting in some plants on somebody else's property — completely uncool.

The guy's property we were growing on had turkeys. Our dog chased his turkeys and he chased our dog, and while he was chasing our dog he found our pot. Then he killed our dog.

Sonny retaliated by putting a sign on the road: *"MD killed our dog."* It really upset the guy and he called the cops on us our first year out. They sent the head narc, Bill Stewart[1], in on us.

So Bill Stewart shows up and I'm serving tea to the head narc of our county, who is asking me questions, and the whole time we've got all this weed underneath the bed in our trailer.

That was our first experience growing pot. We lost our dog, served tea to the head narc and grew a bunch of crappy weed. Welcome to the business.

Why we pursued it is beyond me. It just didn't look like it was going to pan out as far as helping our income at all. It seemed like a lot of stress and worry and not enough return for the time you put into it.

We educated ourselves, met other people and it did eventually work out for us. People started getting less paranoid and started talking to one another. It started to become a community.

Back then we often harvested prematurely because rip-offs and CAMP (Campaign Against Marijuana Planting) were so pervasive. Most of us would start harvesting right around hunting season because hunters or pretend hunters would rip people off. It was very common to at least do a small harvest for insurance. In those days, every gate had a guard and every garden had a guard but

---

[1] Deputy Sheriff Bill Stewart of Mendocino County; he earned the reputation as the most dangerous narc in America.

Mountain Bound

the first weekend of hunting season was always a nightmare.

The CB radios were like party lines in those days. When we wanted a private conversation we would switch to another channel but everyone else would switch to that channel, too. When law enforcement was in the neighborhood, the CB radio was going off the hook with its nonstop chatter.

One year, several of the mothers took all the kids to a rented house on the coast because we couldn't handle the CB radio with everyone all caught up in the hoopla. It made you crazy! There were so many rip-offs happening then.

Early on, it was cops and rip-offs; now it's mold and worms.

Also, we used to have locked gates with combinations we had to change every year. After about August 1st, when the plants were maturing, people often slept in their gardens and no one would leave the hill during that time. We used to ask, "Is there life after harvest?"

I enjoyed growing pot but I didn't like not being able to tell the truth. I think that was why our community became so close; we were all very proud of what we did and believed in what we were doing but we couldn't tell people who were off the hill because unless you were doing it, you didn't get it.

There was also a lot of sensational publicity around growing weed. Bad news makes the news so we were very tight-lipped. Even though it was hard to meet people in the day, it did provide a common bond and nurtured the ability to be open and truthful with our group. But it didn't happen overnight.

We have a daughter and she was never involved in the product or in a situation where her safety was compromised. We kept her safe and away from it because she was a child and didn't need to be part of this aspect of our lives. But on the same note, she was born and raised under the umbrella of being involved in an illegal substance and she learned situational ethics really early. She learned not to talk about what we did in town. She learned it wasn't because we were bad people; it was because it wasn't legal. Early on in her young life, she learned that not all laws are just — that sometimes one must decide for oneself.

Our generation was taught to question authority and, as a generation, we took it to the next level. I never felt guilty about our choice of lifestyle. I had the opportunity to nurture and really know who my child is. There were trade-offs at times due to the illegal aspect of it but it wasn't something that we lived with daily. We just lived our little bitty life, grew our little bitty vegetable garden, and raised our child in a country style that is from days gone by. We were together all the time.

The end result (our daughter) speaks for itself. She is a fine, ethical person with good self-esteem and critical thinking skills.

WHAT DO YOU DO FOR A LIVING?

LILY: The illegality of our business colored us as outlaws. We loved the work and being outside, plus we loved the freedom that it created. But with all of those pluses came a serious minus — what we did was illegal, not a profession validated by society, not something we could talk about with others. Growing marijuana was considered *bad*, and lumped in with heroin, drugs, drug trafficking and all that goes with it.

As we progressed in our business, this stigma hung like a dark shadow and became something that we had to deal with emotionally. It affected our ability to openly take pride in our work and acknowledge our successes. We could only share our pride, our joy, our successes and mistakes with our family and our extended mountain family. When we went outside of this area, we had to parade our token lie of doing something else, because everybody wants to know what you do. For some of us this wasn't as big of a deal as for others.

LOLA: A lot of us had other ways of making an income besides growing pot. We told our daughter to tell the truth — just leave out the part about growing pot. Almost everyone I know up here did some sort of other job so that their children didn't have to lie.

But since we couldn't be forthcoming with new friends, I always felt like we couldn't get close to anybody other than our mountain family. Nobody else really knew who we were and I always had that gut ache that someone was going to find out our secret.

LILY: In this time and this culture, how you make your money is considered an integral part of who you are, and hiding behind another story wasn't a good feeling. There was "town truth" and "mountain truth." You put your town face on, and then you went to town. Done in an honest, caring, open way, I don't think it was emotionally devastating for our children. In my opinion, the pluses definitely outweighed the minuses.

DRIVING TO DRY

Back in the day, we were so paranoid about even drying pot here on the hill, that we used to haul it to a house we rented temporarily in nearby Madrona, hang it to dry and then haul it back here for trimming. That's when a lot of busts were going on here. The sheriff would often arrive with several vehicles in the wee hours of the morning and catch people without any warning. We were growing on our own property at the time and always felt in danger of getting busted. If our garden got circled by a small plane, we would then spend the next several nights in the back of our truck on some absentee owner's property, afraid of law enforcement coming in before sun-up and busting us.

One night Cassie, her husband Hank and I were sitting around trimming pot in the house. It was weird because it was just getting dark and there was a plane circling relentlessly overhead, making us increasingly uncomfortable. Luke had just left to take a truckload of wet pot to the Madrona house.

LUKE: While I was driving out, I ran into that old guy with the long grey hair, named Rex. He said, "You know, there's a game warden up there at the top of the hill at the main gate." I thought, "Oh, what the hell ... I'll just drive right past him." I had a whole truckload of wet pot in my camper and I caught him right at the crown of the hill. He put his hand up, signaling me to stop, and I waved, pretending that we are just waving at each other, and I drove on. It's a good thing we didn't see each other until the last moment because I probably couldn't have gotten away with that. I headed on to Madrona feeling very lucky at having dodged that bullet.

LOLA: So in the meantime we got a CB radio call from a neighbor telling us that the game warden is at the main gate, stopping people and shaking them down, even checking ashtrays and shit. We started freaking because we thought we needed to warn Luke, who would soon be returning with a truckload of dry pot for us to clean.

We'd been trimming and smoking and getting high — and getting more and more paranoid. The plane kept circling above the house. We knew that we had to warn Luke somehow but we were just too stoned to figure out how. My car had leaf and residue all over it so I couldn't drive mine to warn him.

CASSIE: My car was clean but I was also too stoned to drive. I remember that after the plane stopped circling, we found ourselves kind of wandering around outside wondering what to do. Finally we just went back inside and pigged out while we hoped for the best. By the time Luke returned, the road block was gone. What a night that was.

LOLA: Eventually we stopped taking the pot down to the town house to dry, once we realized we could just dry it outside, weather permitting. We would hang it on bailing wire that ran from tree to tree in the thick woods. Luckily, back then the deer didn't eat it; they hadn't acquired a taste for it yet. That came later.

Once we lost a bunch of buds to a wood rat who hauled them down into a hollow tree. Looking down with a flashlight, we could see the nest that he had built with our weed, but there was no way we could retrieve it.

He was certainly using some expensive construction material.

POT SHORTS

JED

Tall, blond and blue-eyed with a long braid, Jed is a mainstay of the mountain community, a man who looks you straight in the eye while really listening. His first impression leaves no question in your mind that he is trustworthy and solid — a good guy. Jed is a builder with a strong work ethic who works and plays fast and furiously. One result of his tendency to move so quickly while multi-tasking is that Jed can't even tell you how many bones he has broken.

JED: I started out in college with a major in mechanical engineering. After three semesters, I just didn't see myself doing that for the rest of my life. I thought, "I'm not even having fun. I've *got* to change this up."

Then I switched my major to business administration because numbers came easily to me and I thought I was interested in advertising and marketing.

After graduating from college, I realized that it wasn't just what you knew, but who you knew. Even though, officially, I wasn't qualified, I became assistant administrator of State Mental Hospital in the Midwest. Apparently, I *was* qualified enough because I ended up with eleven people working under me for three years.

Mountain Bound

I then decided that job wasn't for me. "I can't continue to wear a suit and tie any longer. I have to move — to be outside," I said to myself.

In 1971, my friend and I decided to head to Alaska to work on the pipeline for some big money.

I had a VW bus, so we decided to take our time and turn it into a road trip through California, camping along the way. Then I remembered a friend from college who lived in San Francisco. We needed a place to stay, I found him in the phone book, and we connected.

It turned out my friend had some visitors — dentists from Nebraska who had responded to an ad: "Country Land For Sale." These friends happened to be heading up the next day to the land that they had just purchased. Since it was enroute for us, we followed along and found ourselves outside a small town called Ridgeville.

When we got there, I really liked it. I thought, "It's pretty. The rolling hills, the trees are singing to me ... this is cool stuff! Wow ... these views, these rock formations ... look at all this beauty. Let's hang out here for a little bit."

This is where I stayed. I ended up helping to build structures with locals. Eventually I got my contractor's license, built my own home and started a family.

When I came up to the hill, I knew nothing about growing pot. We smoked it, but had never grown it. Then I started hearing more and more stories about people growing. One guy had about 600 plants growing like crazy in full sun, just over the hill. When I saw this garden, I just couldn't believe that he would have the nerve to grow in the wide open. I thought, "Wow! We can grow our own pot!"

By 1976, I was working part time in the city. That was when I was going to night school for my contractor's license. I did try growing pot, but had a skinny, pathetic little garden of ten or twelve plants.

I had gotten a little taste of it with those few plants. And I thought, "This is really neat, so next year I'm going to do it up big."

My wife Husker and her friend Shannon said, "Jed, you get it all tilled up and ready to plant, and then Husker and I will take it over from there. In the end we'll split it in thirds."

So that's what we did. And they had a 30 plant garden which was hidden back beyond the bushes and couldn't be seen from the house. We harvested about half a pound per plant, growing in a little sun — 15 or 16 pounds in all.

COOPER

And then there's Cooper. He is stocky, has red hair, a big beard and is a sweetheart of a man. Cooper has a huge library of music, loves to dance and loves to garden. As soon as you walk into his lovely Craftsman style house, you understand a lot about this man. His attention to detail and good taste prevail. We've enjoyed many dinner parties at his house, which even includes a dance studio where we practiced for our annual Halloween performances. Cooper never found his life partner because he was always just too damn picky.

I first met him while spending the afternoon with Cassie at Incognito's Airstream trailer. Incognito had just bought a battery-operated blender, which we were excited to try out, when Cooper appeared, seemingly from out of nowhere. "Who is that?" we asked. And I remember Cassie saying. "Oh, isn't he cute!"

Incognito didn't know his visitor personally, but a good friend of his had mentioned he was coming up. So, we just said, "Come on in for margaritas."

COOPER: My friend and I would often drive up to his parents' house in Trinidad, in Northern California. Every time we would drive up there, we would pass a road that led up to this mountain. My friend had mentioned he knew some people who lived up the

POT SHORTS

mountain. Knowing I eventually wanted to live in the boonies, one day we said, "What the hell," and drove up.

Back then I had been told you could grow marijuana and make a lot of money. I just thought, "Oh? Growing marijuana for a living?"

I was still in the system then, working at the post office in Stockton and trying to save money to buy land in the country. Well, after ten more years, I ended up with a total of $5,000 in savings. By then my friend had bought his own place in the hills. He kept saying, "Why don't you come up and grow for me?"

I was focused on working at the post office and trying to sell my house, and then I ended up with less money than I had going into it. Meanwhile my buddy was coming back from his first harvest, bringing pot down to Stockton, selling it to my friends and returning to my house with all this money.

And here I was, having financial problems, thinking, "What's wrong with this picture? I need to say 'Yes, I will go up there and grow for you'."

And that is what I did. I finally just said, "Fuck it."

This friend knew I had been a gardener all my life and thought it would be a good match. So I drove up in my 1970 El Camino — not very appropriate for up there.

Back then the only way you could communicate was through letters. So I sent my friend a letter.

Mountain Bound

He told me to come on up and meet his friend who had the CB name "Incognito." So that was the day I found Incognito's Airstream trailer, right there in the middle of nowhere.

The gate was locked, so I got out of my car and walked up the long driveway. I remember that it was a very hot day.

Then there they were: Incognito and his two women friends making margaritas and welcoming me in. They turned out to be Lola and Cassie. I knew right then, that I wanted to know these people.

COMMUNITY BONDS

JED: Thirty-five years ago, most of the people who came up here were not coming up to grow pot. They were coming up to go back to the land.

After my wife passed away and I became a single parent with two children, and working really hard as a contractor, I thought, "I can't work 65 hours a week. I want to raise my kids and have time with them, go on vacations with them, and really enjoy their formative years."

Lots of us on the hill tried driving into town to work but it is such a long distance. At the same time, we were trying to grow as much of our own food as we could.

We were all growing vegetables, and we thought, "Oh, we could grow this herb, too, along with our other herbs."

It was kind of fun, and we were able to do it, and we enjoyed doing it. And it just so happened that we discovered that we could actually make a living.

Morally I don't have a problem with growing pot because I believe in pot — it's an herb, for crying out loud. I think that if you look at the big picture, you'll see it does less harm to people than alcohol does. You don't want to be giving it to really young people and encouraging use at a very young age but you don't want that with alcohol either. In your formative years you need to be drug and alcohol free and when you come of age you should be able to make your own decisions.

I never let my kids work with pot, trim pot, or do anything with the pot when they were growing up. I always told them, "You're going to college. Once you get out of college, I don't care what you do. I just want you to be happy. If you want to come back here and grow pot, you may, but I want you to be exposed to other cultures and other ways of thinking. I want you to see the potential out there before you pick this little thing where we are living right now."

We all went through the same thing as a community. We all went through the fear while trying to make a living growing pot. We actually came here because it was the "back to the land" movement then. We were anti-establishment, if you will, and I always viewed all my friends and neighbors up here as being in the same boat with me. That's why all my friends came here, too. We were all of the same ilk.

There are a lot of different communities on this mountain but this particular community on this side of the mountain is special. We put together our own school by working really hard to get it off the ground and make it successful — all of us working together for a common cause, for our children, for our families. Normally people go to work and they don't have time to see their kids until evening, but we were able to spend time with our children up here. It's huge how much more time you got to spend with your kids.

POT SHORTS

When I first started growing, I was told by some of the old timers that the number one criteria for selecting a piece of property was water — it's gotta have water or you can't do anything.

Now, with water delivery services, you can buy a piece that doesn't have any water and then put two or three tanks on it and a garden and have your water delivered. Many people put in ponds, which often didn't hold water, so with water delivery it changed the whole game. Properties that were just worthless before became viable, especially to growers.

from start to *hopefully*

finish

POT SHORTS

From Start To hopefully Finish

THE BASICS

LUKE: The process of growing from start to finish has many pitfalls awaiting the inexperienced. For starters, he or she needs to begin with the right seed stock or clone to compete in the current market.

The correct soil blend as well as sun exposure and adequate water are required. Once those are in place one must avoid everything from sow bugs to deer, pigs or bear, mice, rats, voles, and even turkeys. Stock rot, termites and gophers can be problematic, too. More recent problems, which have arisen in part from the use of clones, are spider mites, white powdery mildew, and bud worms. These last three were never an issue in the earlier days.

If using seed stock, the males have to be removed before pollination. There are countless heartbreaking stories of seeded gardens that were useless or close to it, due to a hidden six inch bad boy plant left accidentally in the garden. A hermaphrodite branch (male flowers on female plants) is less common but equally painful.

Once the plants have been tied, supported, and nursed to maturity, that's when the white powdery mildew, stock rot and bud worms become a problem. Mold in the buds are also common and can follow you right into the drying shed.

POT SHORTS

Assuming you have dodged all those problems as well as rip-offs and law enforcement, you still have to dry, manicure, and disperse the stuff.

And it all began at least eight months earlier, so patience is definitely required.

DIFFICULTIES OF GROWING

LILY: Because we lived in the mountains, we had to hike up steep hills, down deep ravines, putting water lines in, and fencing from deer. You name it, we did it.

It was very difficult getting water to those places, tending and maintaining the plants, then harvesting and getting it all out of there.

LOLA: There were many creative ways to hide pot. Most people hid plants under manzanita bushes.

I've heard of some cowboys that grew pot inside walls of hay bales. Because the hay bales were beneath trees, they could only be seen from a helicopter. To get in, you'd have to pull out one of the hay bales.

Another way was to hide the plants inside poison oak. Some more paranoid growers hollowed out a huge mound of poison oak — like a cave — and grew their pot inside that. These guys had worked their asses off to make the top part thin, so the sun could get through. There was a small opening in this hollow, only one way in and one way out.

LILY: In California, you can now grow in the full sun. You're allowed 25 plants, legal, with a medical license. You can drive your four-wheeler or just walk up

POT SHORTS

to your scene. It's so different from the '70s and early '80s.

Besides the variables of the earth and the weather, we have to deal with the two-legged variable, the people, and the four-legged variable, animals.

One year wild pigs were really an issue. And bears can come in and wreck your fences while going after the fertilizer.

It's hard work, which pays off nicely when it does, but you can also lose your entire year's income overnight.

TRIM CREWS

LOLA: After the product is grown and harvested, the buds of the plant are trimmed (manicured until all the leaves are off and you have round little buds and no stems). The buds are either trimmed freshly cut, or hung and trimmed after drying — depending on what the buyers might want that year.

Most growers have a group of trimmers. The number of helpers varies with the size of your crop, and they often work for a couple of months.

It's important for everyone to get along, as you are together from sunup to sundown. Folks sit around talking about everything you can think of to talk about, but one annoying person can ruin the mellow atmosphere of sitting around listening to music and making the buds look beautiful.

I recall one annoying trimmer, for example, who would hum really loudly when the group was talking about something of no interest to her. Most of the time, though, we really got along and would just grow closer. We talked about everything under the sun, from your most embarrassing moments, to family, to past or future dreams.

There is usually some drama, a few really hard workers, someone lazy, and of course many stoners and your token alcoholic. Most trim groups live and eat

POT SHORTS

together — taking turns cooking meals and helping with all the other daily jobs that need doing.

Trimmers often live with you, as they may have come to work from some distance. I remember one crew that had a member from Chile, one from Thailand, France, and of course, California and Oregon, all on the same crew.

Some growers will pay a trimmer by the pound while others pay by the hour.

Paying by the pound is often more cost efficient, as you'll have really slow trimmers and really fast ones, and some might not care how much product they get done when paid by the hour.

However, if you pay by the pound, you might be unfortunate and end up with someone like Gory — a guy who would always grab the biggest buds, and then conveniently take a lengthy bathroom break when the small, lighter ones, were still on the table.

For many years it was just our close friends coming up to help out. After the trimming, you package up one-pound units making sure to get the moisture content just right. Too dry and it will fall apart, too moist and it will mold.

Nowadays, trimmers are seen everywhere in pot towns, hitchhiking and holding signs saying, "Have shears, will trim."

From Start To hopefully Finish

After the trimming, you are ready for the scariest part of the business — selling the product.

TO TRIM OR NOT TO TRIM

LILY: The people who thought up trimming should be shot. It's a serious waste of energy and product. The buds should just be picked, the big leaves cleaned off and there it is. It's another one of those shiny package ideas that now we can't get out from under. What we now have to do with the buds to meet people's expectations is not real — it's unnecessary and a huge expense for us. It should be marketed differently. The upside is that it's a great cottage industry, creating jobs for tons of people.

But it's also like watching paint peel.

SUSIE (LILY'S DAUGHTER): When I was a kid, I remember people were trimming in a very disorganized fashion — like into wicker baskets. Everyone was cleaning just their own pot and doing it in their living rooms — doing the country cut. Now I've heard stories of people who have had special trimmer tables built with desk cutouts and holders for their scissors and cups and special chairs. And they're hiring professional chefs to make all their meals. It's gotten pretty ridiculous — like an assembly line in some places, but in other places they're still so disorganized it makes my skin crawl.

LILY: Your dad and I used to trim, just the two of us. Sometimes, we'd have our mothers and grandmothers come. It was in our family, and we'd just work and visit until it was done. But now it's transitioned out of the mom and pop situation into traveling trimming crews who go from scene to scene and make their living doing that. It's become more professional — more honored as a business than a party favor.

POT SHORTS

FLEE!

LOLA: Before the choppers, law enforcement only had fixed wing aircrafts to spot the pot.

Their plane would often circle our garden and we would freak-out and dive into the bushes or a ditch and hide.

They would usually send a convoy up within the next few days, so everyone would listen closely on the CB radio to determine where the convoy might be going.

Our friends, Jerry and Rube, used to come up often, and sometimes helped us trim in a little shed below our house, leaving one of us in the main house to monitor the radio to learn if the convoy was coming.

We would then run down to tell the trimmers that law enforcement was in the area. If they were coming in our direction we would run down the hill and hide in the bushes until we heard that they had turned down some other driveway and it was safe to come out.

I have this great memory of Jerry, who was very funny and very gay, running down the hill waving his hands in the air yelling in a high hysterical voice, "Flee! Flee!"

It became a great joke for many years to come.

From Start To hopefully Finish

RIP, my dear friend.

SELLING THE PRODUCT

Lily and our friend Monty were hanging out after a road meeting. I asked them how they would explain to someone that was not in this business of growing pot, how to sell it.

MONTY: Well, if you are fortunate enough to make it through harvest with a crop in hand, you are then faced with the uncomfortable task of selling your weed.

LILY: Yes, you then have to take it to market and, needless to say, our marketing style is very tricky because of the illegality of it. How we involve the middleman and how we get our product to the consumer is very squishy — it's really the weak link of our business. You know, "Let's do business for X amount of dollars in the dead of night at the side of the road," with yahoos who look like they couldn't count to ten.

Until you establish your own trade circuit, which most of us do very rapidly, you find yourself often dealing with people you wouldn't give the time of day to — certainly you wouldn't allow them into your home. Then, here they are, knee-deep in your home and in your personal business.

MONTY: Usually you would know someone who knew someone you could sell it to. Often you would

From Start To hopefully Finish

have to take a cut in price because the person who turned you on to the buyer wanted a cut, too.

Sometimes you would find a cashless buyer and you would have to front the product — hopefully seeing your cash eventually. That is a painful waiting game which has led to so many losses it makes you shudder.

Or you might get lucky and meet someone with good connections and cash in hand. Someone almost too good to be true would get you to worrying that he may be a narc. Or what if he were a legitimate buyer who might then get busted and flip on you?

It was very satisfying to have cash in hand eight to ten months after sprouting the seed.

LILY: Maybe at some point in the future, it will be more like selling soybeans or corn, and we can focus on farming, not marketing — but for now we have to do both.

MIDDLEMEN

I was talking to some guys I met at a party that live down the mountain a bit, and they were discussing how much money they made selling their first pound back in the '70s.

DIRK: I remember distinctly: $800 a pound. And it was a big, beautiful sensimilla that I grew in the greenhouse in the backyard.

That was the first pound I sold. I sold it to some dude who ended up growing a lot of his own in Sonoma County. He had a big outdoor scene; that was back in '74 or '75.

We were still working in the city and that's when I decided we better think about this growing some more.

JJ: My God, that's a good price for back then. The first pound I sold, I got $400 and I thought I had cut a fat hog. This was 1977.

DIRK: It went from $800 straight on up. I never looked back. Of course, now we're starting to look back.

JJ: I remember when it was 8, then 12, then 16, then 18, and every year it ratcheted up.

DIRK: $4,800 I topped out. I know there were people who topped out at the 5 + mark. You might have been one of them.

JJ: That one year, we probably sold 8 to 10 pounds at $5,600 a pound.

DIRK: Wow, what year was that?

JJ: Let's see, it would have been the early summer of '93, selling pot that was grown in '92.

DIRK: Interesting. I remember when Bernie used to buy it back then, put it in jars and fill up cases of canning jars. He had that whole *Amway* thing going on.

If anyone sold to anybody that he knew, he felt he deserved a cut. If he brought them up here, then you owed him a percentage. It was all about connections. I moved a lot of weed for friends, but never expected or made money doing it.

JJ: Being middlemen is never fun. That *Amway* thing reminds me of a story.

One day, while I'm working on a house, Joey stops by and asks if I have any pounds to sell. Says he has a buyer for 4 pounds.

Next day he picks up the pot and pays me the money. *Badda-Bing, Badda-Bang.* No muss no fuss.

A few days later, this guy named Tim comes by and asks, "Hey did that thing work out?"

I said, "What thing?"

He then says he should get $200.00 a pound of the four pound pot deal.

He claims that he knew the buyer first and had introduced him to Joey.

"The buyer was my guy," Tim said. "So that $800.00 I owe you? We're even now." Then he drove away.

camp

POT SHORTS

THE UNLAWFUL SIDE OF UNLAWFUL

Zoey: During the "Just Say No!" Reagan years of the '80s, an all-out assault by the government was conducted against marijuana. Innocents were caught up in it as well as growers, all dealing with frightening behavior with helicopters and armed agents swooping onto private property.

Lola and Luke's community grew strong bonds partly because of the proclaimed "War on Drugs" and the danger it created for them.

They did not have access to mainstream legal protections but instead had to fend off all manner of personal property thefts, rip-offs, and attacks from fringe elements, as well as from Federal Agents. So they bonded.

Lola: *"We got our CB radios. We had look-outs, guards, booby traps, and other defenses. We were ready at the first call to come to the aid of a friend."*

They were not aggressive but found themselves cast as defenders. They only recognized the good this herb could impart as a high. It stimulated peaceful feelings and was a portal to sensual, pleasant experiences. It was alcohol and prescription drugs that were killing people.

But, be that as it may, they were under attack.

POT SHORTS

After many chilling experiences, plaintiffs in Humboldt County filed a Federal lawsuit and submitted 50 declarations with sworn testimony of the harassment, intimidation and outright theft they were experiencing. This court document reads like a TV crime movie, except that the "bad guys" weren't the peaceful, back-to-land families. They were the cowboys and the renegades the government hired to carry out the new Campaign Against Marijuana Cultivation (CAMP).

Judy Rolichek described in court how a CAMP team of about 25 armed officers surrounded her home, ordered her family out of the house with their hands up, and held them at gunpoint for 2 and a half hours while conducting searches without a warrant. A family dog that was merely standing and barking was shot and killed by a CAMP agent.

Many declarations were made that involved helicopters hovering within feet of people's windows, angling so they could look inside — at people in bed; a woman in an outdoor shower; and, in the case of Charles Keys, at home with his 5 year old son, while in an outhouse:

"Four helicopters in a diamond formation came within a hundred feet of our home. The largest one put its nose about 100 feet away at my eye level, and hovered watching me while I was on my toilet. I didn't move, so he moved right above me and blew the toilet paper away. My son and I left the property, as I feared for our safety."

Rebecca West described another instance:

CAMP

"There were 4 of us women and 2 children standing in an unfinished area of our partially completed home, visiting. The helicopters suddenly came roaring over the hill, over the treetops, sweeping down like stuntmen. I thought they were going to go right through the building. You could see their faces.

"One then landed nearby and 3 armed men jumped out. We were scared to death. The two ladies we were visiting told us we should take our children and go.

"So we took off running. One of the helicopters flew real low, chasing us about a quarter mile. The children were screaming!

"The armed men held the remaining two women at gunpoint. Still other agents conducted a fruitless search."

John Reilly had served as a helicopter crew member in the US Army. One day his home was buzzed by two CAMP helicopters at an altitude of 100 feet. He said, "They appeared to be using tactics similar to those I observed used in Viet Nam to terrorize the populace."

A pilot who was low on fuel was heard on his radio being advised by another pilot as to where he could land.

"You could land up by that house, but the fellow has a camper shell propped up."

"That's OK; I can just blast the camper shell down the canyon and land."

"Do what you want."

POT SHORTS

The Deputy DA testified that the helicopter pilots were selected primarily on the basis of their flying experience and ability to "manipulate" the aircraft. They were private contractors with no law enforcement expertise.

The Court concluded that they were "habitually engaging in some sport of their own."

After dozens more of these testimonies, and with no repudiation of any import, the Court recognized the validity of the case and issued a preliminary injunction to stop the activities of CAMP.

Numerous other residents could have testified as to the scare tactics and harassment that was much too common.

......

Decades later, multi-agency task forces still use helicopters as their #1 tool to combat the weed industry. Over the years they have become more professional with their incursions. Generally speaking they now seem to avoid close contact with homes when busting gardens.

CITIZENS REACT

CASSIE: Remember when the helicopters flew down the center of downtown Garberville as low as they could, right down Main Street?

It was "Let the games begin"... as if the official season of CAMP'S intimidation was open. I think that was around the time the Citizens Observation Group (COG) was formed.

LOLA: A representative from the COG organization came and we had our first meeting at our little community school. They even gave us these little "COG" patches to sew onto our clothes.

If someone was getting busted, we were supposed to film what we saw. This was during a period of especially high CAMP activity. We were hearing so many stories about CAMP and other law enforcement acting like wild west outlaws ... shooting dogs, taking personal belongings, not using search warrants ... basically harrassing and intimidating. COG made us feel like we were doing something to protect ourselves.

There were many complaints that the National Guard were tresspassing on private property, which they always denied. I took a video right out of our window showing the National Guard hovering at eye level with a huge military helicopter. The big Huey was so close to the house that they were looking in the window at us.

POT SHORTS

We didn't have pot on our land but they were taking out weed on a neighbor's land. They were supposed to be clearing out National Forest land but back then I think they had better luck finding it on private land.

I ended up taking my video to that big pot lawyer, Ron Sinoway, who was representing a lot of pot farmers at the time.

I remember thinking, "This is going to be *gooooood!* They can't deny this."

But nothing ever came of it.

GATOR: Another time they came over from Trinity County to raid here. They would pop over into our county randomly, then disappear. Apparently, they were not supposed to be here.

They used CB handles, too, and we recorded them. We sent the recording down to the local newspaper. This would prove they were out of their jurisdiction.

I wanted to be anonymous so I just let them have the tape. I have no idea if anything ever happened with that but it was on record that they were doing cowboy raids ... out of county and without authorization.

CASSIE: Some of those choppers liked to play cowboys and mess with people.

They did that to our friend Lori. She became hysterical and was screaming.

CAMP

I heard the guys on the police scanner and they said "Leave that woman alone! She's going to have a heart attack!"

Lori was in her garden and they started chasing her, flying right near her while she ran in a panic down to the little creek. They were thinking it was fun to chase her.

We heard the officer say to the pilots on the radio, "You need to stop chasing her!"

GOLDIE: The other chase like that was with Tiny and Deb.

They had their garden down in the canyon. When the heli came in they started running up the hill. Tiny got up the hill but Deb couldn't go any farther.

Deb said, "They got right on me so I dove into this poison oak bush. I lay down in there for a long time until they finally left. I actually crapped my pants, but they didn't catch me."

CASSIE: Back then the radios we had were big with large antennas. I had leaned ours up against the fence.

I heard helicopters coming and I got scared, grabbed the radio and started running. Only I didn't run for the gate; I turned and slammed right into the fence. Just like a deer.

By the time I got home I felt pretty sore … and stupid.

CASSIE: Remember when we were all sitting out on the point at your place, Gator, in the meadow looking down on the canyon below your house, watching the choppers hauling out nets of pot?

We heard them on the radio and scanner, talking to each other. We could tell it was Lori's water lines they had found and cut. Then they found our water lines and tore them up.

GATOR: Yeah. Then I saw them flying out with a wheelbarrow and a rototiller. I'm looking and looking. Then I realize, "Hey, *it's my wheelbarrow!*"

They took it all the way down to Rex's, loaded it, and flew away with it.

LOLA: I think that was the year I was so impressed with you and Goldie. The year you lost everything.

You guys said, "We still have sex. Sex is free."

EAGLE EYE

JED: The whole process has evolved and changed so much. In those early days, you never wanted to grow in the open where the plants could be seen.

Law enforcement used fixed wing airplanes to spot plants in the open. Then they would come to make a bust. And every single time it would be this convoy of county vehicles — not SUVs — just squad cars, and perhaps a pick-up.

Old Stevie was a big grower off Lake Road. They called him Eagle Eye. We all had our CB names then.

Eagle Eye's job was to be the lookout on Snag Ridge at what we call Gus's, on the big, grey rock there. He'd set up camp with his thermos of coffee at first light every morning, and he'd sit there until 10:00 a.m. If he saw the caravan coming up the road he'd put the word out on his CB radio.

Then you would hear the CB just come alive. People were checking on their partners or their guards and trying to get the word out to anybody who might be in danger in their gardens.

You would also see people scrambling out to the different lookout points to see who might be getting busted or where the convoy was going next. Most people didn't get much done in those days as it was so nerve wracking to have law enforcement all over the place.

Then in 1980 or thereabouts, law enforcement got lucky. They had tried busting pot growers with helicopters over in Hawaii — calling it Operation Green Sweep — and they were really successful.

After that, they said, "Let's take this show to California."

So from 1981 on, it was helicopters, and it was serious business.

LUKE: That's when they started using long cables to drop lawmen directly from the choppers into the gardens and haul out the pot using a net attached to the cable. That saved a lot of time and energy trying to get vehicles close to a garden.

It was amazingly efficient and so depressing to watch.

HUMAN NETS

When the choppers would come up to do a raid, they would usually set up at the same place. It was a level spot on the main road before you entered our community. It was a private piece of property where they could land easily. It could accommodate a couple of choppers, a dump truck, lots of vehicles, and many troops.

CASSIE: My favorite helicopter memory is when we were helping Luke harvest. You would often hear on the CB radios when the choppers were coming in for a raid. Then they would arrive dramatically and circle.

We knew what that meant. They were going to be coming back with the troops.

So we headed over to help Luke. We all just pitched in and as fast as we could we just hacked and dragged. We mounded it up on the back of his little Toyota pickup. I mean mounded like a mountain! It was just slash and drag.

LOLA: We were rough on the weed in those days and, in retrospect, we really abused the plants. Luckily buyers wanted anything and they weren't particular like in today's market. There was large bud, medium bud, and pinch bud and the strain wasn't important.

CASSIE: That's right. That one day we could hear the *PHWIP PHWIP PHWIP* coming. I remember that I just threw myself on top of the haystack, spread eagle, arms and legs across the plants, face down. I literally was on top of this haystack, in the back of the truck holding on for dear life. Luke was driving up deer trails, dodging trees, because there wasn't even a real road then.

I was just crushing the bud, but we were getting the hell out of the garden with the goods.

I will never forget it.

LOLA: That was the way we had to harvest sometimes, because we didn't have nets with us to hold all the plants in the trailer or truck, so we were the nets.

I often thought what amazing pictures these scenes would make, but was too paranoid to take the film to be developed. That was as recent as 10 years ago. We were still doing that under their noses.

We were still hacking and rolling burritos[2] just 10 years ago. The comfort zone that we feel now is new.

---

[2] *Rolling burritos*: Throwing pot in tarps and rolling them up in order to move them.

TOO SAD TO WATCH

LUKE: Here's a helicopter story I just remembered.

Years ago, down by the river, we had the mother of all gardens. The whole creek was full of it. It was easy to spot but difficult to remove, due to the steepness and narrowness of the canyon.

Unfortunately law enforcement had an answer. They brought in a very small two-man helicopter, much smaller than the usual aircraft.

Myself and my intelligent partner, had harvested about one third of the garden days earlier and dragged it up hill in many locations to dry, making sure that we left no trace of leaves behind that anyone could follow. We intended to return and haul out the much dryer and lighter loads later but here came the helicopter.

Dipshit, my other partner at the time, tried to go down there and rescue the rest of the weed without talking to us first. He ran ahead of the two CAMP cops and cut and dragged weed up to the same locations that we had already hidden weed.

In the process, he left an easy to follow trail for the cops.

After watching several loads fly out, we decided to go to town to avoid the painful sight of all our hard

POT SHORTS

work going up in nets. When we returned, I was told they worked most of the day down there.

We went down the next morning and found that they not only removed all the green weed, but also found all of our dried and hidden weed, because our partner Dipshit had his head screwed on backwards.

FIRST YEAR

Monty is a handsome dark haired man with an average build. He loves to write and is a bit of a hermit. He graduated with a degree in psychology from the University of Alabama and is the son of a preacher man. He worked in the mental health field and did some part-time landscaping jobs until his friend offered him a job growing pot.

He said "I jumped at the chance, looking forward to an alternative lifestyle and becoming part of the wonderful community I had visited so often."

Maggie is his wife. She is a loving, beautiful blonde that loves animals and children. She had also worked in the mental health field as a psychiatric technician and was working part time as a real estate agent.

MAGGIE: My best friend lived on the hill and I would go up there and trim for her. I would have liked to move up earlier but I was waiting for my daughter to graduate from high school.

MONTY: I remember my first year up here. You know that song that goes "I left a good job in the city, working for the man every night and day?"

Well, this was the song I was singing before I moved to the mountain. I was fortunate to have hooked up with, and eventually worked with Magoo. I learned a lot about a lot of things from him. The major thing I learned was that growing pot is not a sprint; it's a marathon.

So my first year had been a long hot summer hauling dirt and amendments to God-forsaken places where goats wouldn't go. We were transplanting, digging holes, deterring deer assaults, choking off gopher attacks, and poisoning the occasional grasshopper infestation, not to mention keeping our fragile water system up and flowing to our plants.

Everything was looking really, really good that day in early October. All the plants were getting close to harvest. Oh, that stinky, medicinal smell … it was going to be a good harvest.

Tank, my other partner, just pulled up to the garden to check everything when we heard *"the sound."* That horrible, gut-wrenching sound only a helicopter makes. We hesitated for a second, not knowing what to do.

The sound got louder and louder. This just cinched it for us to start hacking. No sooner had we started hacking when the sound started to fade and disappeared altogether.

Great. Now what? Were they gone for good, or were they coming back?

The garden was very small, but we decided a little bit of something was better than a lot of nothing.

CAMP

So we hacked and tarped and hid that big burrito down a ravine and got the hell out of there.

We then made our way back to the other side of the mountain, only to find a helicopter hovering over our other garden at Magoo's. As we stopped on the road to watch, the helicopter dropped down out of sight, only to be replaced by another helicopter rising from below. It was impossible for them to land so they lowered men down to the garden on cables, with a very large net attached to another very long cable. We were getting hammered, and hard.

We watched the full nets go away while listening to the sound of the straining helicopters barely clearing the tops of the trees.

I lost pretty much everything that day. But also as the song goes, "People on the river (hill) are happy to give."

With a lot of help from Magoo and a good community, my wife and I pulled it together to be back the next year and every year since.

That was twenty years ago. No regrets.

BAD ROLL OF THE DICE

JED: I'll never forget that one year ... we had braved and weathered the entire season and it was the last freakin' day of work for CAMP in the entire county.

And it was even the *end* of the last day, like 5:15 in the afternoon. We thought for sure it was all over.

And then one of these choppers flew over once. My partner Sonny and I had cut most of our garden and hung it over the fence. The very last nets of the last day of the season, and they flew over and saw pot drying on the fence.

So they dropped in and took everything we had worked so hard for.

That was just a bad roll of the dice.

IT'S A BUMMER PLEASE

JED: One year CAMP came in and took out my little garden early in the summer.

After scouring the mountain looking for replacements, I got 12 plants from a friend and replanted in the same location. I had also just performed this Herculean task of planting on a steep bank above a creek — God-awful mountain goat type shit.

Just when I had that whole garden in and had replanted the other one, CAMP came and took out both. That was the only place CAMP came on the whole mountain that year — my two gardens.

······

MAGOO: Another year, on the last day that CAMP was working, I was just about to sit down and eat lunch after cutting down some nice plants and hanging them on my fence. I wanted to let them dry out for 24 hours so they wouldn't be so heavy.

Then, *BOOM!* A chopper comes over the peak from Jed's — real low. It comes up over the garden and I drop everything and run down to a lower garden and start cutting whole plants. *Chop! Chop!*

I can hear the CAMP guys working just above me on the upper garden. I cut 10 to 15 plants and throw them over the fence when a second chopper comes from another direction, just sitting on top of me.

I jump the fence and grab the big bundle that I cut, and I run into dense woods as he continues to follow me. I then run smack into a hornet's nest and get stung and scratched and bruised and pissed off, but I finally lose the chopper.

CAMP gets all that was left except a small bundle because I think 60 pounds of wet weed was too much for the chopper to lift. It was CAMP's last stop. Bummer that it was me.

......

LUKE: Yeah, I remember one day we were pinned down in a garden.

This time we were not cutting but just waiting it out. Too often we would cut and run, so this time we were in there just waiting. The helicopter and all their guys were below us working, cutting a neighbor's garden down.

Then the helis came right over the hill, super low. All we could do was drop down in the garden, under a pot bush. They could see us perfectly.

There was a thin manzanita canopy, and they were only thirty feet off the ground. We were pinned down in a pile in the garden, all three of us huddled

CAMP

together and the chopper was so close we could see their faces and feel the wind from the rotor. I remember putting my hands over my face and looking between my fingers so that I could see them without them seeing who I was.

As soon as they bugged out to get the ground crew and the cable we cut as fast as we could, then dragged it across an open meadow and into the thick timber where we could hide.

The chopper returned quickly with a crew and landed just as we got safely to the timber. They took everything we left, which was most of it.

Usually we regretted cutting too soon, but this time we guessed wrong, waited too long, and lost.

CUT AND RUN

MAGOO: I remember this one time ... I think it was late October.

Frosty and I had been out checking our garden when we heard a chopper. All of a sudden it was right over us really fast and just stopped and hovered.

I'm like, "Check it out, Frosty. We've got to get out of here."

Frosty yelled, "No! We've got to get the plants out of here now!"

And he just started hacking so hard I thought he was going to hack his hand off.

I was trying to hide behind the tree so the chopper couldn't see me, and to wait to see what they were going to do next. We had also heard another chopper about a quarter of a mile below, so there were two of them working the area.

As the chopper started to move away, so did I, and then he came right back over me. Maybe my bright white t-shirt caught his eye. He moved right over top of us as low as he could but there was no place for him to land the chopper.

He left, but I knew he had seen me and he would be back with a ground crew and a net. That gave us just enough time and one opportunity to harvest the garden.

CAMP

We worked fast and furious so by the time they got back, it was gone and so were we.

POT SHORTS

INFRARED

LUKE: Being chased by choppers got to be commonplace.

I remember the first time I got shaken down with that one with the infrared camera under the front of the heli. It was the latest state of the art technology.

I thought that all I had to do when the helicopter came over the ridge top was hide.

I'm in the only garden in the area and hidden under a thick canopy of white oaks. He comes over the ridge heading parallel to me and suddenly turns straight toward me. I'm like, you know, "Why straight here?!"

The next thing I know, I'm behind this oak tree and he is over the top of me. How did he even know I was there? I mean, the garden's totally hidden; I'm hidden.

It was the infrared camera. He could see that I was the only human on the hillside and came straight to me.

I'm like a squirrel scurrying around this big oak tree, trying to stay on the opposite side from him. And he's going around and around trying to get a better look at me. The wind is blowing the hell out of me and I'm freaking out because I'm only 50 yards from my garden.

CAMP

After they harassed me like that for about five minutes, they flew over the garden and then buzzed off.

That night we ended up moving the entire garden, I'm sorry to say, because they never came back.

JED: That night I moved a whole garden. too, working until about 9:00 a.m. the next morning. My back hurt... everything hurt... I felt like I had been hit by a whole fleet of trucks. And they never came back. I've moved gardens way too many times. I'm done moving gardens,

LUKE: Can you imagine how much damage they did that one day with that heli with the infrared on it? Five minutes on me and on you, too, Jed. They probably did it all over the county. Can you imagine how much shit was pulled up, moved or cut down?

The infrared was a damn effective tool. That chopper really had fun workin' us over that day.

JED: And people would say, "What's that funny little thing sticking out of the front of the heli?"

Well, it's the infrared. And it was a different looking chopper than we'd ever seen before. That year they staged at Big Lake and had three friggin' big choppers. *Three!* They had this whole landing pattern set up there — one direction they would take off from, and one they would come back to.

POT SHORTS

That was the nastiest day ever when they had three choppers in our neighborhood. Those were the bad old days.

rip offs

POT SHORTS

BOOBY TRAPS

Ranger Danger was a character on the hill who loved to make contraptions. He had been ripped off many times so he was constantly creating different types of booby traps to catch the thieves. I asked him one day if he would describe some of them to me.

RANGER DANGER: I've tried many booby traps to hopefully prevent a rip-off. One was a siren that would sound off when someone walked into the garden. I used a mouse trap as a switch and two or three 9-volt batteries that ran the siren — the higher the voltage, the louder the noise. On some later models, I used light switches instead of mouse traps, but they both worked just fine.

I had lightweight fishing line painted black to prevent it from being visible, and it went to the mousetrap switch which was connected to the siren, then placed high in a tree to avoid being turned off by the thief. Therefore, when a thief entered the garden he'd get tangled in the fishing line and set off the alarm.

I never caught anybody but it did chase off some kids who were in the midst of stealing a crop of immature plants. They apparently didn't even care that the plants were not budding yet. When they got to the third plant that was rigged to the alarm, they triggered it and skedaddled out of there. I heard it hours later — still going strong with the gate wide open and three pulled plants lying on the ground.

......

Another time the siren went off but it didn't save us. This strange gal by the name of Shorty led a crew of brazen meth heads up into my garden. I found one perfect, very small footprint on a fresh gopher mound, confirming that it was my speed freak neighbors, including this gal with really small feet. The next day, I confronted her and measured her foot — which was a perfect match.

She of course denied it and there was nothing I could do. This group took every plant, every bud. It must have taken all night because they actually used pruning shears. And they liked my alarm so much they took it with them.

......

Another trap that I was glad never got put to the test was one I called Swami's Bed. It was made with a number of wood screws going up through and sticking out of the top of the plywood. I carefully placed it in the garden, camouflaging it with leaves. But I was the only one who accidentally stepped on it. And, luckily, the 3 inch screw went through my shoe and between my toes instead of directly into my foot. Because of the difficulty

Rip Offs

I had removing it from my shoe, I'm now relieved that it never caught a thief.

One of the first gardens I planted back in the late '70s was stolen in July when it was knee-high with leaves and no buds. But to some rip-offs, it was weed, no matter what stage of growth.

I imagine their thinking was, "This stuff's worth something. Let's steal it."

And so they did.

......

The following year I added an elaborate security system to my newly planted garden. A friend had a camera with a timed shutter on it — high technology back then. I borrowed the camera, soldered a small brass arm on it and camoed it in a brown paper bag up in a tree, aiming it at my best and biggest plant. Black monofilament went from the camera to the plant so that when the line was pulled it would trip the shutter. A few seconds later, the arm would complete an electrical circuit that went to a black powder charge attached to the tree six feet below. The idea was that I would get a photo and the thief would run like hell when the charge went off.

I got this whole thing set up. I'm up there in a madrone tree, barefoot, trying to be really careful to skirt around the fishing line. I took a couple steps and caught my toe on the fishing line, just enough to trip the shutter accidentally. And holy shit!

POT SHORTS

All I had time to do was cover one ear with my hand and the other with my shoulder while I hung onto a limb. I was waiting in a panic for the boom of an explosion just six feet below ... and nothing happened.

The little timer arm that would complete the circuit to the black powder charge rubbed up against the paper bag and stopped 1/8 inch from completing the circuit.

Wow! So I just had to calm down and reset it, which I did. Luckily it never got tripped by a thief that year.

......

The year after that I decided to just put the black powder charge on the back side of the tree, about 10 feet high and far enough away from the plant that it wouldn't hurt anybody. It was the same system but without the camera.

Weeks went by and I was sleeping easy knowing that the explosive alarm had me covered, when in the middle of the night — *KABOOOOOM!* It went off and shook me out of bed.

Naked, I jumped into my cowboy boots, grabbed my shotgun and flashlight, and ran down the hill, panting. Throwing the beam of light on my best plant, I saw it was still there.

In the morning, I realized what had happened. I didn't peel the insulation back far enough on the wire

Rip Offs

and the heating and cooling off every night of the plastic covering caused the wires to eventually make contact — a design flaw.

......

I remember another booby trap I had before I moved up here. I had a little garden in my backyard near town, and I put razor blades in the stalks of plants to deter thieves. But instead of thieves, the sheriff came to the door, saying someone reported marijuana in my back yard.

I said, "Yes there is, officer."

And he said, "Well, let's go pull it up."

So I got ahead of him and said, "I'll pull them up." I was pulling as fast as I could so he wouldn't notice my diabolical trap. Even while trying to avoid the blades, I cut the shit out of myself.

About that time, I heard him say, "What the hell?" and I looked back to see him holding out a bloody hand.

I'm apologizing and explaining that the blades were meant for rip-offs and not for him. He was a pretty nice guy and luckily I got off with a warning.

......

I think my favorite booby trap was a hornet's nest. While checking a garden once, I noticed a fairly

POT SHORTS

large, grey paper nest hanging about four feet above the ground. I knew the type of hornets were bald faced, because I had been stung by them in the past. They are large, black and yellowish white, and very protective of their nest.

I carefully tied a fishing line to the poison oak branch which they had built their nest around. They were checking me out and even bumped me on the head a couple times, their way of giving a fair warning.

I ran the line to a nearby plant. If anyone tried to harvest the plant, it would shake the shit out of the nest, something the hornets do not tolerate. It was probably the only time I actually hoped a rip-off would show up but none did.

RIPPED IN THE BOONIES

LOLA: It was always disappointing to lose your garden. But losing it to CAMP was far less painful then losing it to a rip-off. When CAMP took it, they were just doing their job. Losing it to a scumbag rip-off, and knowing he was profiting from your hard work, was very hard to deal with.

We didn't like growing on our own property because it was just too scary.

A good friend had about 200 acres of land and wanted us to grow for him for a percentage. We jumped at the chance. His land was way out in the boonies, farther out then we were, and we had to drive a couple of hours to get there. Once we arrived, we had to pack multiple bags of fertilizer, fence material, shovels, drip line for irrigation, and everything else we needed on our backs and hike for another half an hour.

We used to go up there once a week and work from sunup to sundown, always getting badly eaten by mosquitos. We worked so hard in the heat that we looked forward to taking a bath in the creek and then splurging on dinner at a tiny restaurant called "The Mad Creek Inn" on the highway home.

After following this laborious routine for several months, when we finally came up to harvest everything was gone. The plants were just skeletons with no buds. It looked like a graveyard. We were heartbroken.

    We never figured out who it was because it was out in the middle of nowhere. We decided some hunters must have stumbled on our plants and believed it to be their lucky day. That was part of the business, though. Getting ripped off or "Camped on" was quite common. Having a harvest or not was always a total gamble and this time we lost.

GUARD NOT

JED: I remember about five rip-offs, but it would be too painful to tell them all.

There is one that really sticks in my craw, however, and that was when Sonny and I had a garden together over on this one property. We did things a little differently back then — we'd do just one big harvest.

Sonny and I walked in one Friday afternoon and mentioned to each other that it was really getting close. And this was one time I wish I would have listened to him.

"I think we could harvest today," Sonny remarked.

"You know, once we start it's just going to take too long," I answered. "Tomorrow is Shannon's birthday and I really feel like I have to go to Garberville to honor her day. Let's not do it today but on Sunday morning. We'll party tomorrow for Shannon and then I'll be up here bright and early Sunday morning. So, first thing Sunday morning. OK?"

Gory was our guard then. Sonny and I went back on Sunday morning, as agreed, and we've got our loppers, we've got our Coronas, we've got our bags and all our stuff. We walked by the trailer and there's Gory

POT SHORTS

sitting there with his flip flops on and his feet, propped up, just reading a book.

"How's it going, Gory?" we asked.

"Just great. It's a beautiful day," he replied.

We kept going up and got to the top of the hill. And there was not one single plant left, or even part of a single plant. We couldn't believe it. We were just sick. Well you know, in that situation you don't know what to do so you just start looking.

We started making circles around, and bigger and bigger circles to see if we could find a lead or sign going anywhere. Finally, about 120 yards out, we found this area in a little cove of trees where they had processed it all.

In other words, they dragged the plants over there and clipped all the buds and ends and good shit off, and probably bagged it there. And then they took it.

We looked and couldn't find any evidence so I said I'd come back with my horse to look a little farther, ya know. The next day we searched from early in the morning until almost 6:00 p.m. that night.

We didn't find a single thing. Then all of a sudden I thought I'd better go look at my other garden — the one on my own property on the other side of the road.

I went to check it out and some SOB had gone in and topped the ends off the whole garden. Only these pinchy-ass little things were left standing. All the good shit had disappeared.

Rip Offs

I was never so angry with Gory, the guard, as that year. And he got ticked at us for being mad at him for not watching the garden.

That guy had such an attitude — no remorse. Needless to say, Gory doesn't work here anymore.

SNIPPER

LUKE: We had many complete and partial rip-offs in which the thieves would take only what they could carry on their backs.

I remember this big Silver Haze garden we had that was getting cut by someone other than us. When I mentioned this to my partners, they said, "No way."

So I suggested that we make only diagonal cuts just above a right-branching limb and see what happened. Sure enough, after we cut, we found many other cuts that we hadn't made. So we cut again, careful to clean up all the rip-off's cuts, and sure enough, we found the same thing when we came back.

We should have hired a guard, but didn't know of one. We kind of suspected our neighbor's friend who was temporarily staying with him. He would know when we were coming in, as he could hear our bike approaching. Because of this, we got ripped-off up until the end of the season. I think the thief never suspected we knew we were being cut on since he continued to rip us.

He got away with it because the garden was so big. He was one lucky scumbag.

STAR WARS

JED: The worst was my guard Sam. I went on more wild goose chases with that man.

I'd get a call at 10:00 p.m. I'd be in bed, and he'd say, "Oh, Jed... there's a rip-off going on out here! You got to come help me! Oh, my God!"

I would crawl out of bed, check it out, and there would be no one there.

LUKE: I don't know how many times this recurring theme happened — back when everybody was sleeping in their gardens and watching for rip-offs. The stars looked like they were traveling through the trees and the guards would think they were seeing flashlights. How many times did that happen?

It fooled Julie for years and years and never did stop fooling her. She just couldn't get a grasp on it.

"But it was there!" she would say. "And then it was there! And then it went out."

JED: One night Sam had me meet him out at the end of our gate. He looked across our road to that steep hill to the left of the lake and told me he saw vehicles up there in the bushes driving across this clearing.

I replied, "Man, do you know how steep that is for a vehicle to traverse across there? It would roll over."

He says "I tell you, they're up there!"

Just another star ripping us off.

Rip Offs

HOME INVASION

This incident took place at Ziggy and Drew's house. Ziggy first came to the hill as an acquaintance of Cooper. At that time, Ziggy had never seen a marijuana plant. Ziggy was following Cooper to his garden and had to crouch through the manzanita bushes to get there. Those were the days when everybody grew in manzanita bushes or under the trees.

CASSIE: My husband Hank and I got a call that there had been a rip-off and it was bad. So we rushed down to Drew and Ziggy's like fools.

We didn't know what to expect and didn't even have a radio to call for help. We just heard that Drew had been ripped off — someone had held him at gunpoint and tied him up — and he had just gotten loose. If we had had to confront someone, we would have been in trouble but the guys who had done the rip-off were gone and Drew was beside himself.

When we got there it was all over. They had basically taken everything.

HANK: Well, it happened around daybreak. It was foggy and somewhat rainy. It was still more or less dark out and everybody else was sleeping.

The intruders had come in over the fences and into the house wearing ski masks. The hinges were cut on the gate. The first alarm had been somebody kicking in the door while everyone was sleeping.

They broke the door into pieces and held all the trimmers who were staying in the house at gunpoint. They tied Drew up, threatening to kill the dogs if they didn't stop barking.

Two of them had on Sheriff's Department caps, according to Drew. I figured they were probably ex-military because they used a police home invasion format. Drew said they were communicating by walkie-talkies with someone down at the garden who was complaining that the crop was too small.

One guy kept admiring the taxidermy and wanted to take it. The other guy told him to shut up and leave it alone. They were talking to each other about supposedly going to a number of properties. So it sounded like it was someone local, a neighbor perhaps, who knew the area.

CASSIE: And the whole time they were stealing and ripping off, they basically had Drew and two other men handcuffed or tied up. The three dogs continued to bark so they made Drew lock them in the other room.

HANK: They had tied people's hands with zip ties behind their backs and it took Drew almost an hour to get loose. They took all the wallets and thought they had taken all the phones.

I know it was really traumatic for our neighbors to go through all that, but it did kind of bring our neighborhood together more. We were pretty fragmented at that point. And that episode is what spurred everybody to buy good radios and to get more organized.

NOT VERY NEIGHBORLY

LUKE: I went to one of my grow scenes one day and found buds were cut. I followed footprints right out of my garden to a grow next door.

A guy we called Crank had hired a low life from Sacramento to tend his garden. They had shitty, late weed so they stole mine. I followed his foot prints right to his camp.

Not knowing what to expect. I went home and got a friend and returned. When we confronted Crank's worker, he denied it, but after a quick search I found my weed.

JED: I remember that. I was one of the group that showed up later to run him off the mountain after Crank refused to make him leave. We took some photos of him so we could show them around the neighborhood as a rip-off. He never came back.

LUKE: Crank said he would reimburse me, which he eventually did. He left some moldy import trash weed with a friend to give to me.

......

LUKE: There was another band of knuckleheads from L.A. camping down on some property a couple of big ridges over from there.

Rip Offs

They didn't know how to grow. They were doing everything wrong. They had all the water they could have wanted, a gushing well and a big spring. They didn't know how to contain it or deal with it or manage it.

Instead they had a big crew of Mexican laborers chop down trees with machetes and dig huge holes in horrible rocky soil and line them with plastic. They pumped from the well into the plastic lined holes, and then ran the water through huge PVC pipes to all the poorly chosen garden sites that had to be cleared of trees. It was painful to see such a complete brain fart in progress. The environmental damage they did was horrific.

We were growing right next door, a nice fat garden and were worried that they might rip us because theirs was so puny. Sure enough, that's what they did.

We followed the drag trail from our ripped off garden a half mile through their scene to where they bucked it down small enough to put in garbage bags.

They had just harvested their little pissant of a garden and then focused on ripping us off.

They were long gone to LA by the time we found out. We wondered if they were singing the Arlo Guthrie song, "Going into Los Angeleeze, bringing in a couple of keys."

GUARDIAN ANGELS

LOLA: Everybody used to have guards in every garden and some of the people in the community would chip in to have a guard at the front gate that was off the county road. In fact, the community even had a trailer hauled out there for them to sleep in because most of us had lost gardens to rip-offs or CAMP. But nowadays nobody seems to worry about rip-offs.

JED: We've always had guards until this year, but generally it's not as common anymore. However, it's amazing how many younger folks aren't even interested.

They just need to lose their garden once.

LOLA: We have always equipped our guards with radios and told tell them to call and let us know if somebody is in the garden. They are not to confront the rip-offs, just get out of there. We have such a great neighborhood watch thing going here that everybody comes running to help.

COOPER: One time, as an example, we had a couple of friends who came up from the city to guard a garden. I told them to get CB names, but it never occurred to me to tell them to choose tough names. They called on the CB saying, "Maple and Fern."

Rip Offs

I bet everybody got a kick out of that. One morning at the crack of dawn Fern said he heard some footsteps and saw two people walking towards the garden.

One walked towards them with a pistol, saying, "Don't move."

Poor Fern and Maple took off running and thank God they didn't get shot.

The gun toting thieves ripped off the garden, but by the time we heard about it and returned, they were gone. That was the end of Fern and Maple's guard career.

POT SHORTS

NIGHTMARE WITH MISTER JONES

Jesus, Butch, and Olive are friends that live on the outskirts of our community. After our community soccer game they started telling me this horrendous story that happened a couple of years ago on the Jones' land. Mister Jones' grandfather, who lived in Oakland, owned the property connected to them, and over the last 30 years, they had never seen any sign of him. Apparently his grandson found out about the property and decided to pay a visit.

JESUS: We've talked about the fact that it wasn't uncommon for people to grow on absentee owners' properties if the land was nearby. Regarding the Jones land, there were several growers bordering his 40 acres. Four different growers were growing a little bit on his property.

BUTCH: I didn't know at the time that maybe 30% of our garden was just slightly over the property line. We were growing on another neighbor's and paying him, but we didn't know exactly where the corners were with Jones.

OLIVE: We weren't used to seeing anybody up there, and noticed a trailer had been moved up and a couple of black kids hanging out on the Jones piece.

One kid was found wandering around and the people asked, "Can we help you? Are you lost?"

Rip Offs

He said he was looking for a store for cigarettes. But the closest store was 55 minutes away on a dirt road.

Then we found out that the kids were just dropped off by Mister Jones to watch his place. I went over there and tried to be neighborly and brought the kids some veggies. They were just a couple of young kids.

About a week later a bunch of older guys started coming up and staying there. They were carrying guns and just hanging around on Jones' property. They obviously knew that there were a lot of plants being grown there and we all assumed they were just waiting to harvest them.

JESUS: I had this whole garden being grown there. I thought that rather than being reactive, I would be proactive.

I went over there and asked who was in charge and the kid said, "You need to talk to Mister Jones."

I see Mr. Jones is there, so I went over to him and said, "Look Mister Jones, I'm growing on your property. You can have it if you want it, but since you guys probably don't know how to do it, I'll follow through. I'll grow it and then give you a cut."

Mister Jones said he'd think about it and somehow he came up with this magic number of 35 pounds. We passed that number back and forth over a couple of different encounters and finally he said he wanted half of what we harvested. I figured that was fair in order to avoid any violence.

POT SHORTS

OLIVE: One night, we woke up in the middle of the night with all this gunfire going off on the border of our property.

We were hunkering down inside the house because it was so loud and went on for a good half hour. We thought they were shooting at us!

The next day, we decided we needed to go talk to them about it.

JESUS: It was scary — really scary. Butch and I, who don't have guns, went up there to talk as rational, reasonable people. Mister Jones was nowhere to be seen, and this guy they called Mad Dog approached us.

BUTCH: He was carrying a sawed-off shotgun and pointing it in our direction.

We asked to see Mr. Jones, and he said, "Mister Jones is not available right now, you'll have to wait."

So we waited another 20 minutes at their camp which was a scene. It was really dry, and the middle of fire season and these guys have got a campfire going. It's hot and dry and sparks are flying.

The campfire scared me more than the shotgun because if it got out of control some people were going to lose houses and gardens.

I eventually got to talk to Mr. Jones and explained to him that we were unaware that about 30% of our garden was on his land but he could have that 30% and we would even continue to tend it for him. He agreed but after a few weeks we notice that his guys have taken a big cut including much of ours.

Rip Offs

We realized we had to do something or lose it all. So we waited a couple of days and went back when only two unarmed guys were there, and we took what was ours.

The two guys said, "You can't take that. Mr. Jones is not gonna be happy."

I said we made a deal and were sticking with it.

JESUS: So the next year, we did not grow on Mr. Jones' property. However, the Jute property that Butch used to grow on next to Mr. Jones was for sale. A guy named Dickie bought it.

Dickie had a 215 certificate to grow medical marijuana, so he proceeded to put in a garden, and everything was going well until one Saturday morning.

I was working down in my shop when Dickie comes flying in on his four-wheeler.

"Jesus! Jesus! You gotta come help! They're ripping off my pot right now!"

"Who's *they*?"

"Jones' guys."

"How many?"

"There's four or five of them anyway. They're doing it right now. You gotta come help me!"

So, naively, I thought, "I have talked to these people before and maybe they'll listen to some reason if I go over and talk to them."

POT SHORTS

So I get in my truck and head over. As I'm coming to this wide spot in the road, I look over and there are three vehicles parked there with two huge bundles of pot on the ground and three guys walking into the bushes.

"Hey, stop! Mr. Jones, is that you?" I yell out.

I get out of the truck and Mr. Jones turns around, pointing an automatic rifle at me and the guy behind him has an Uzi — also pointed at me.

"Hey, Mr. Jones, we need to talk," I say. And he just stands there.

Mr. Jones, still pointing the AR15, has on shooting glasses and a bullet proof vest, and the guy behind him is pointing the Uzi, and in the bushes I see a third guy with a shotgun.

"You can't do this — it's not right," I said. "This pot belongs to Dickie who has a medical need and has worked very hard to grow it. It's been grown on his property and you're stealing from him, Mr. Jones, and it's just not right."

So Jones says to me — and I'll never forget the words, which are burned into my memory — "'Less some of you motherfuckers wanna be killed, just get out the way and let us do what we do."

I looked at their faces and their eyes and thought, "I'm not reasoning with anyone here."

So I just turned around and calmly walked back to my truck and took down a description of the three

Rip Offs

vehicles and the license numbers. I then went straight home and called 911 and told them the truth.

Naively, again, I thought, "Okay, they're on their way up here to help us out even though it might take a couple hours."

Thinking the cops were coming to our aid, I went back up there and waited with Horse and Dickie. Yes, Jones and crew were still down there, and yes, Dickie was unsuccessful in talking them out of his pot.

"Don't worry; the cops will be here any minute," I told them as we anxiously waited.

But then I realized, if the cops don't hurry, they were going to get away. I hopped in my truck and went back down the road, thinking I would block it and they couldn't get around me.

Sure enough, in about 10 minutes, they had broken the gate and pulled it out of the way, trying to get out. The lead vehicle had Mr. Jones and another man. Jones honked and honked and I just stayed put.

He started yelling out of his window, coming closer and closer.

"Get out of the way or I'm gonna ram ya!" Jones screamed.

"Shoot," I was thinking, "I don't want my truck dented. I'll just drive really slowly."

If I turned right, they could turn left and escape, and as I'm driving, Jones keeps trying to pass me, but I keep him from passing. He's honking his horn this whole time, and I'm driving as slowly as I can.

"Maybe the cops will be at the gate," I thought.

I stopped before the magnetic sensor so the gate wouldn't open, but he started going around me. It was a real scramble out on the county road. I kept whipping left and right so he couldn't pass.

I was thinking the whole time, "Where are the cops? Where are the cops?"

No cops. I was just sweatin'.

And then when we got out to the ridge, I saw reflections from windshields — many cars reflecting lots of light.

"Oh good, the cavalry's here. We got 'em. Piece of cake. We got 'em now."

There were like 23 law enforcement vehicles — not only county sheriffs and highway patrol — but BLM, Fish and Game, and Cahto Indian tribal vehicles. It had gone out over the radio that an armed robbery was in progress and they were intending a roadblock, so they called for all available help in the area.

They had cars lined up and guys standing out there with rifles and shotguns aimed right at me, the lead vehicle. They didn't know me and thought I might be a bad guy too.

"Stop the car! Get out on the ground. Get your face in the dirt. I want you to EAT DIRT!"

Rip Offs

"But I'm one of the good guys," I replied, while on my stomach with my face in the dirt.

I knew they were stopping Mr. Jones and his friends too. They got Jones on the ground, and behind them was a pick-up truck with a huge bundle of pot — maybe 15 to 20 huge plants, a six-foot bundle, laid down flat. Mr. Jones was in a brand new Lincoln Navigator. Behind that was the pickup and behind that was a Mercedes Benz with two more guys.

So lots of law enforcement, a bunch of interrogation, and then I kinda told my story.

Everybody was lying in the dirt and they had handcuffs on the other guys when Dickie drove in. So they started interrogating the bad guys and me, and then after I told my story, Dickie told his and I think they jived.

Then they got us together and were asking us questions, like, "Why are these guys up here?"

They searched all the vehicles and they found the camera and the tripod that the Jones crew had used to videotape the entire rip-off. Jones was still wearing his bulletproof vest and his shooting glasses but they didn't find any weapons.

Dickie volunteered to lead law enforcement back to their motor home, and sure enough, they found six weapons, five of which were illegal. There was an automatic rifle, an Uzi, a sawed-off shotgun and two more illegal guns that were confiscated. So they got the weapons, they got the pot, they got the videotape, and they took them all down.

Jones and his pals had made quite a production of filming the entire rip-off by using a VCR camera on a tripod at the edge of the garden. Every one of them was in their camos or other bad-looking getup, sporting a weapon. One guy had a mask on. Whoever was filming would zero in on one guy who'd look real bad for the camera.

They were found with that tape, the camera and the pot. The guns were also found — and they were all acquitted. The DA chose to not even take them to court.

In my opinion, the DA at the time was way too soft. They had me down there for a preliminary, like being in court, and I had to testify in front of everybody. The DA's office wanted to go over this whole thing.

"Mr. Jesus," they said, "We want you to see this."

The camera started rolling and they showed a video that Mr. Jones had put together and he was doing this scam of selling shares to pot gardens.

They had a picture of Mr. Jones with a suit on, and he was onscreen telling how you could multiply your money by ten. If you invested $10,000 with him he would give you a share in a legal marijuana garden. He called the whole thing "Elysian Gardens."

They had music going in the background and a picture of Jones and another worker out in the fields,

Rip Offs

going from plant to plant to plant. And they were huge plants.

Looking closely, I could see that it was *my garden*! The whole thing was my garden from the previous year, but I didn't tell the DA's office that. The whole scam was Jones on the internet trying to get investors to give him $10,000.

So then they took me for a walk to identify the confiscated weapons. We went into this well-guarded room and I had to confirm the identity of the AR 15, the Uzi and the sawed-off shotgun.

They then said, "Well, okay then ... we're going to nail these guys."

And that's the last I heard from them.

Jones and his crew never got a day in jail.

bad juju

POT SHORTS

BAD BOYS

LUKE: One evening, when I was deer hunting up on a high rocky peak overlooking everything, I heard voices. I crept up closer and overheard two teenage kids talking about how easy it would be to rip off a garden — one kid trying to talk the other into doing it. The more I listened, the more angry I became because I realized they were probably more of Benedict's foster kids, and he had already brought up other teens who had been caught ripping people off.

These kids almost shit in their pants when they got up to leave because I was standing right behind them holding my deer rifle.

After I gave them a heavy scolding, I went to Benedict's and unloaded years of pent up anger. He had not only brought up thieves but he apparently once tried to molest a boy who I picked up hitchhiking. Turns out the boy was one of his foster children and was trying to escape Benedict. There is something seriously wrong with the system if a guy like that can foster a bunch of teenage boys.

I had told the boy when I was giving him a ride that he needed to turn Benedict in. And soon after that incident, the sheriff gave him a visit and he was no longer able to have foster kids at his house.

POT SHORTS

A few years later, another of Benedict's teens — now a young adult — came up.

Big Billy called me on the CB and said, "I think someone might be ripping you off because there is this strange pickup on the road near your grow scene with large cardboard boxes in the back."

Lola and I headed up to see what was up. We got there and sure enough there was weed in the boxes and two people were coming up the hill carrying more boxes. Lola got on the CB and called for backup. When they got to the truck, I'm calling them on the rip-off. Next thing this guy pulls a knife and starts getting cocky while moving in my direction.

I had my deer rifle in the truck and went for it right away thinking, "Shit ... I hope I don't have to use this."

Lola, who's pregnant, gets on the radio again and tells people to hurry. Fortunately, when they saw the gun they lost the cocky attitude. And people started showing up. It was amazing how many people came.

Once we had plenty of people with us, we started going through the rip-off guy's truck. We found his briefcase and an unmailed letter he had written in which he was actually explaining how he had made all this money pulling the green, and even bought this nice truck.

After we read the letter out loud to everyone there, we all talked about the best way to handle the situation. There were so many neighbors by then —

Bad Juju

most of whom had been ripped off many times — and our anger was mounting.

It was decided that he was less likely to return if we roughed up his truck a bit. So several people wrote *"thief"* on his truck and trashed it to the point where it would still get him down the hill, but barely.

That rip-off never came back, although I wouldn't be surprised if he continued doing it somewhere else.

It was amazing how many people came to our aid. Talk about your neighborhood watch.

POT SHORTS

TOUGH LOVE

LUKE: Another rip-off in our neighborhood involved the Shyster teens. The parents kept a rather low profile but the teenagers would run amok — taking out gardens, mine included.

But they went a bit too far when they broke into Rosenbloom's trailer and busted it up, destroying stuff and stealing canned food.

What they didn't figure on was Rosenbloom's mom. Like a good Jewish mother, she wrote all the expiration dates on the cans before giving them to her son. When he found his trailer busted into, he was just red hot — so of course he went looking around the hood and found his mom's dated cans in the Shyster's house.

The teens were already suspects because of my garden getting ripped off during the same time frame. Not only had they just been seen in the area, but we had suspected them before. Every time they came up to their property for vacation, pot was missing from someone's garden. So, rather than go to the father, a well-known asshole, Rosenbloom decided to send a message. He went to their house — a single story built on tall posts on a steep hill — with the plan to knock out all the posts and let the house crumble down the hill. He started in the middle with a sledge hammer and then worked his way towards the outside. When he carefully knocked out the last few posts, expecting it to fall any second, the house still stood there. Rosenbloom had overlooked a few posts in the middle, and the whole thing was balancing perfectly on just those posts — almost defying gravity.

Rosenbloom knew he couldn't go back under the house without killing himself, so he left it that way. I guess when that asshole Shyster came home and saw his house just inches from destruction he must have figured out that his run-amok teens had brought on the revenge, especially since Jed and I had confronted him earlier about them. He must have straightened those kids up because it was the last time they messed up. He clearly understood the "tough love" message Rosenbloom had sent him.

OLD MAN AND WILD HUNGARIAN WOMAN

CASSIE: Hank, my husband and I, were growing a garden one year with an old man and a wild Hungarian woman. Because the choppers were hovering in the trees right above our garden on one afternoon, we knew they'd be back in the morning. So we told Old Man and Wild Woman that we had to harvest that night.

Their son was a sheriff, so they couldn't get caught growing on their own property.

Since we had to take out the crop early, we didn't get the yield we had anticipated, Wild Woman got pretty upset with us. "What? What happened to the money?" she asked. She was one mad Hungarian.

And that was the same year she shot her husband in the lung. We knew that shooting her husband wasn't an accident even though they said it was — because she would never carry a gun, never touch a gun, never have anything to do with a gun. We actually went to them and asked what really happened.

When they stuck to the story that she was carrying the gun and tripped and shot him, we said, "We don't believe that. That's not true."

After that, they didn't want anything to do with us — and it was a blessing because we had been feeling

Bad Juju

responsible for helping them and making sure they had money coming in. They were kind of like our parents and we helped support them.

But after that confrontation, the wild Hungarian put a curse on me — and she went around telling people I had stolen from her. When we were building our house and the carpenters were around, they said she actually came here searching through the house.

Later that day, I saw her driving towards me out on the road, so I stopped in the middle of the road, got out, and stormed up to her car.

"Look," I said. "Any curse you've put on me is going back on you tenfold. You're in trouble! You stay out of my home!"

And that was it. I never had any more problems with her. I'd see her at the post office and she'd look away.

She ignored me until the time when I couldn't get pregnant, and then she began telling people it was because of her curse. She was taking this whole thing way to the extreme, literally telling people that I was a thief and we had done all these bad things to them.

POT SHORTS

So when their house came up for sale, you better believe I talked a friend into buying it. I told him I would be the best neighbor he ever had. "You watch my back and I'll watch yours." I was so ready to get rid of this crazy woman.

WIGGED OUT

TOBY: We found this note in our garden that said, "You stole our water which equals 20% of your garden," and that was about how much we were missing.

First Luke got on the CB radio, angry as hell and tried to call Wiggy but he wouldn't answer. Luke says on the radio, "We're coming up Wiggy!"

We jumped on our motorcycles, drove up there and said, "This is bullshit. Why the hell did you take our plants?"

He said it was just what they had coming to them as compensation for the stolen water.

We said, "What are you talking about?"

He said, "Well, you took that water from my property,"

Beth, his skinny little wife, came out with her .38. I could look down the barrel and see the nose of the bullets.

LUKE: Wiggy was standing in the doorway and I was watching Beth's hands shaking, while holding that .38 revolver and aiming at my chest. I'm red hot pissed, and should have realized the danger but didn't at the time.

I'm demanding he come down off the deck and talk face to face but he wouldn't budge.

POT SHORTS

I know he had his hand on another gun just inside the door, and after a lot of hot words we decided to leave. The whole time his whacked out pistol-packing wife was pointing that shaking gun at us.

Wiggy had put property line flags on a due magnetic west course without using the proper declination which is about 18 degrees. His 18-degree mistake put our water on his land, and in his mind we owed him 20%. We pointed out that he had used the wrong compass heading to establish the property line but it's hard to reason with a knucklehead. We decided getting shot wasn't worth it so we left.

CASSIE: I was driving to town one day and saw Wiggy hiding in a fir tree by the side of the road. I could see his feet and a leg hanging out of the bottom of the tree. I turned around and realized it was him, and he was hiding. The guy is kind of creepy.

Another time, we were having a spring dug on our property but were close to the property line next to Wiggy's property. Wiggy came at 7:00 in the morning and woke me up, yelling at my front gate.

I said, "What happened, what's going on? Do you need to use my phone?" We had one of the only phones up here at that time.

I went out to the gate to meet him, and he was going on about the water and the property line.

I said "I don't know what you're talking about. Is there a problem with the property line? If there is, when Hank gets home, he will handle it. He's in the hospital right now."

He said, "I know."

I said "What? You know he's in the hospital and you're in my face about a property line?"

He was totally trying to intimidate me and scare me. I thought, "This guy's a dangerous man."

TOBY: And stupid, too, because he doesn't know you.

CASSIE: I chased him all the way up my driveway and up the ridge, throwing rocks at him.

When he had his place up for sale, I told a friend who wanted to buy it, "First thing you have to do is get a surveyor because Wiggy will lie to you about where things are." So my friend paid a surveyor to come in there and survey the whole damn thing, and his report didn't agree with where the stakes were because Wiggy had moved the stakes.

That's one way to acquire more property.

POT SHORTS

HOG-TIED

Dante didn't grow up on the mountain, but he had friends that lived here. After he graduated from college, he couldn't find a job in the city, so came up looking for work.

DANTE: It was 1999 in October and harvest had just begun. I was heading home, coming from my pot garden and was stopped by two Sheriff's Deputies. I was in my work clothes and didn't have my license with me but did have the registration for the vehicle. They told me to step outside the vehicle. I did and they searched me and found some trimming scissors in one of the pockets of my shorts.

When they were frisking me, they had said, "If you can show me a driver's license, we'll let you go. Take us to your house."

I didn't know what to do at the time, to tell them I lived at my friends on the mountain, or my place in town. They then handcuffed me with my hands behind my back, my ankles were tied, and they put me in the back of their sedan, all for having trimming scissors and no driver's license.

I was staying at a tiny little place at Jake's house, a nice man who had also loaned me his truck. I didn't want to bring any harm his way.

I thought, "I'll just take them to my house in town."

They kept saying, "Where do you live? You have to live somewhere back here."

I said, "I'm going to take you home, back to town."

They got extremely pissed off, cussing at me, saying they were going to go up every single driveway saying "you're going to put other people in jeopardy," because they felt they had the right to go on any property looking for where I lived.

They pulled up to several gates and got out and tried to unlock them. Most people don't have their addresses on their gates, but Jake did on a wooden sign and they saw the address the truck was registered in. The gate was locked so they rolled the windows up, and this was on a day that was about 100 degrees out, and they left me there.

The sheriffs hopped Jake's gate and they started walking down the driveway.

Jake happened to drive up and saw I was in there. He started whistling for the sheriffs. The doors were locked, so I had to stay in the car.

The sheriffs came back, asked Jake a couple of questions. They then followed Jake up to where I lived on his property. Jake went into the house but he couldn't find my I.D. and they wouldn't let me out to get it.

Back when they were frisking me, they had said, "If you have somebody identify you, we'll let you go."

POT SHORTS

So I told them, "Listen, here's my friend, he's identifying me, it's his truck, everything is okay here. I'm not stealing the truck."

They said, "No, we're going to take you in and arrest you."

I was so frustrated. They took me to town, booked me at the county jail. They never even read me my rights.

Jake has a clean record and does a lot for the community. He called the head sheriff at the time, saying he was a concerned citizen who pulled up to a sheriff's car and saw a young man hog-tied in the back of the vehicle.

He noted it was close to 100 degrees with the windows rolled up, and said "I'm wondering, is this how you conduct business with people, whether they are guilty or not? I don't believe they should be hog-tied on a hot day with the windows rolled up and nobody around."

He left a couple of messages, wanting to talk to the head sheriff to say his piece for the record.

I was in the holding cell with a few other people. I didn't get bailed out until midnight. I had a court date to see if charges would be filed, and nothing was filed.

I'm guessing that Jake's complaint had something to do with setting me free.

wild life

POT SHORTS

ROAD KILL FOR DINNER

LOLA: Luke was always doing things that I was just not used to, but I loved that about him.

One time when we were driving on the highway going north to our cabin, my parents, who were coming for a visit, followed us in their car. The plan was to meet up at the Ridgeville gas station. Then Luke and I saw a car hit a deer and the car just kept going.

Luke pulled over right away and saw that the deer was dead. We threw it in the back of our truck and drove off the highway under an overpass. Luke pulled out his pocket knife and quickly cut the hams and back straps — the best part of the meat — off the deer, leaving the rest for the buzzards. For Luke, there is no reason to waste good meat.

We drove back up on the highway and caught up with my parents at the gas station. My dad said, "Gee, we thought we were behind you."

And Luke replied, "Yeah, but we needed to make a quick stop for dinner."

That was one of the things they loved about him: He was such a good provider.

WARDENS, GROWERS AND BEARS, OH MY!

LOLA: Remember when the game warden came up here looking for bears? Some grower had killed two bears that were rumbling in his greenhouse — fighting over fish emulsion and destroying his plants. It was a bummer he killed the bears, but then a guy named Benedict called the law, giving them a good reason to just cruise around up here, looking.

When they were cruising around, they saw Magoo and followed him into one of his gardens. He's like, "Oh, hello," and they took him off to jail.

When we heard that evening that Magoo had been arrested, Luke went over to the garden that he and Magoo had together and just cut everything.

LUKE: I cut all the plants and dragged those huge hog bushes into the deepest woods. I whacked away all night, chopping down this monster of a garden. Paranoia was surging through my body. I thought that since he was arrested, they would come back in the morning and find the rest of the plants, and he would be in even more trouble.

Lola headed down to post his bail and told him I was cutting down the garden. At the crack of dawn, I hear Magoo's voice. "Hey, Luke, stop!"

Wild Life

But I had just cut the last plant. I could only say, "Magoo, I'm sorry. They're all dead."

"Oh, no." was all he said.

Magoo really got screwed. When they arrested him, I guess some cop said, "So, you were going to hand some ounces out to your friends and maybe sell some too?"

Magoo said, "Yeah, yeah ... right," sarcastically.

He signed the police report, a kind of semi-confession that they had written, and he must not have read the whole thing. This made it very difficult for his attorney to help him.

Magoo had talked to the police, they put it on paper as a confession, and he signed it. Remember, anything you say, can and will be held against you in a court of law.

He paid his attorney $7,500, and had to take a drug diversion class in town for ten weeks. He finally got it expunged from his record.

......

MAGOO: On another occasion, my partner Bobby called me, out of breath, saying, "My money has been stolen! I went out to the barrel. The lids were off, bags gone."

So I said, "Okay, I'll be right down."

POT SHORTS

It was in the morning and I had to get dressed. Just as I was going out the door, the phone rang again.

It was Matilda, Bobby's wife. She says, "Hey, we found it."

I decided to go down there anyway. Matilda had found the bag of money about 200 yards from the buried barrel with chew and bite marks on it. We had cleaned up some blood and bone meal bags and threw them into the trailer and Bobby had walked through that and had stood there burying his money. A bear must have smelled his tracks. You could see where the bear had been rummaging around in the bone and blood meal and you could follow his tracks to the barrel.

The bear must have gotten a fingernail under that lid and just popped it off. *Boom!* Popped that lid right off and got a foreleg down in there and snagged it with a claw. He then pulled the bag up to his mouth, sunk some teeth into it and walked off about 200 yards to set it down. We found the bag just where he dropped it.

You would think, "No way a bear got into it ... it's a screw on lid."

Well, they've got can openers on their hands. If the bear had taken the money far enough away and we had never found it, we would have thought someone was watching us in the woods and we'd have been suspicious of everyone we knew.

......

Wild Life

LUKE: I had a bear incident that was pretty obvious. I had four metal garbage cans, stuffed full of weed and duct-taped shut, with camo net over them, buried in leaves.

A bear had found them and pulled them into a ravine that had water running down it. I found them all jumbled down there in the water with bite marks right through the cans in several places and the lids stripped off. The weed was strewn up and down the ditch and through the culvert — floating — the packaged pounds broken open and filled with water.

At that time, we didn't worry about eating and packaging simultaneously, but after this incident, we started worrying about it because all it takes is a hint of food scent and they go for it.

This was a bummer for us. We had to bring everything inside, put the fans on and bring out the heaters.

Back in the day, there was even a demand for brown weed — which is the color it turns after getting wet — so it wasn't a huge loss. Maybe we could have called it "Brown Bear Kush."

......

LILY: One afternoon I was going out into the woods to tend my little patch, way far away from any facilities — and I had to poop.

POT SHORTS

So here I was, pulling my pants down, getting all nestled in and ready to do what you do, and I looked up, and about 15 to 20 feet away from me was this big, cinnamon-red bear coming through the woods. She hadn't seen me yet, but she looked up, and I was right in the middle of my process at this point and there's really no stopping it. She was just looking at me and then she just stopped.

And I'm looking at her, going, "Shit, shit, shit!"

No kidding. Then, just all of a sudden, she probably got a whiff of it. She just turned on her heels and ran the other direction. And I was just going, "Thank you Jesus. Thank you Jesus."

I hopped on my bike and I was on my way.

And of course I couldn't help thinking, "Does a bear shit in the woods?"

Wild Life

IT'S NOT BAMBI ANYMORE

LUKE: For years we hung our pot out in the woods without a problem. But that all ended when I lost a mother lode of weed to deer. We then began making these huge bundles and hoisting them high up in the trees with a pulley. My brother would be up top, tying off the bundles, until the whole tree was full.

MAGOO: I had never had anything eating on my lines, plants hung from baling wire strung like a clothesline, so I never hoisted anything up any higher. We strung baling wire from tree to tree over deer beds for years.

But somehow they keyed in at some point and started liking the taste of it. I've had them eat everything hanging down below five feet.

I remember when the deer were ravenous and we only yielded maybe three pounds — we were growing in the shade — out of a hundred or so plants. I dreaded checking plants; more got eaten each night.

We threw bird netting over them and the deer just ate basketball-size holes in the netting to get to the plants. Eventually they just hammered us — possibly because of a decline in grazing land. Eight or ten plants would disappear each night, and after we got the fencing up we found big dents in the fence where they were trying to get through.

POT SHORTS

One guy, while moving some of his starts into his station wagon, left his doors open. When he came back he found the deer eating the plants right out of his bags in the backseat. Once they try it, it's on their menu.

I also recall Jojo being so frustrated with the deer mowing down his plants that he built a platform up in this tree and borrowed one of my rifles.

They were so stealthy in the dark that he would say "I can hear things snapping. I know they are there, but I just can't see them. I'm standing up in my little crate in the tree, shooting the gun to scare the deer ... and they got six more plants last night."

He was so frustrated.

LUKE: I used to spend the night down in the garden because of that. One doe that behaved like a pig would root under the fence. Once she got in there, she liked what she was getting and just kept coming back.

I just couldn't seem to intercept her.

MAGOO: Yeah. I recall once dozing off in a hammock. This big buck got within a few feet of me, made a snorting noise that scared the shit out of me and I fell out of the hammock! Then, "*galoop galoop,*" he went running off into the brush.

I hadn't heard him sneak up at all.

it's a mixed bag

POT SHORTS

BEING IN TOWN

CASSIE: Here is something stupid I did.

When my mom died I had to go meet my family at a court appointed negotiation of the will. I had to be at court in Sonoma County for at an exact time. Well, at the time, we used to haul some of our pot down. Since I was in a hurry because of the appointment, we just stuffed the pot into a black garbage bag, tied it up, and shoved it down in the cab of our little Toyota pick-up truck.

At this point I'm running late and I'm really rattled about getting to this meeting because my siblings were already uptight at me. And then I get to the Santa Rosa Courthouse and can't even find a parking spot.

So I'm like "Shit, shit! What am I going to do?"

I'm just driving around, and driving around. I think, "Okay, that's it. I've just got to park."

So I park in a No Parking space. I lock up the car and decide to leave the wing windows open to help keep the heat out. It was mid-day and hot. So, I go in the courthouse and have to go through this whole thing with the family — sit and talk, and talk. I'm just sitting there hoping that the truck doesn't get towed. So, after it's over, I'm hurrying back, trying to stay cool because my family — well, we don't talk about any of this. I get back and look and ... thank God, the truck is still there.

POT SHORTS

A lot of sheriff cars are there, too.

It's around the change of shift for the sheriffs so they are all there. I open that cab, and it was just — WHAM! The smell was that intense. I just got in the truck and drove away as fast as I could.

......

GOLDIE: Gator had some pot in his car one time when we were visiting his sister in San Francisco. His sister lived two blocks from the Presidio in San Francisco, which was a military base at that time.

When Gator unloaded the car he put the pot on top of the car. Then Gator and his nephew went to get a pizza on the other side of town. So he drove through the Presidio to the other side, he got the pizza, drove back and then said, "Where's my pot?"

They both just looked at each other. So he got back in the car and started driving back — and **it was right there in the middle of the road!!**

GATOR: I'm thinking, "Where are the MP's?"

I'm sure they must be watching me. "There's the box in the middle of the road. They're just waiting for someone to grab it."

But I grabbed it and got out of there. I was lucky.

......

It's A Mixed Bag

LOLA: I remember Rascal bought a Japanese maple at Friedman Brothers, put it in her car, and went to another store next door. When she returned to her car there were a couple of security guards and some people looking in her window. Someone had called the security and told them there was a pot plant in her car.

She came out and said, "It's a Japanese maple for heaven's sakes."

......

LUKE: Years ago, while driving south on 101, I noticed a police car close behind me. I had gotten a couple of speeding tickets recently, and I had a couple of joints on me, so I was careful not to be going over the speed limit. About a half a mile later, the cops light goes on so I pull over.

He asked to see my license and asked if I knew why I was being pulled over, and I replied, "I have no idea."

When he told me I was weaving I realized what had happened. I laughingly replied that I had lifted one butt cheek to let out a fart and may have moved off center just a little.

There was no sign of humor on his face when he said, "In the future Mr. Luke, I recommend you stay in the middle of the road while passing gas."

POT SHORTS

I damned near got a ticket for farting.

It's A Mixed Bag

GREEN SOUP

MAGOO: Remember the time we were crossing the creek by the gravel pit? As we were driving you glanced up and saw something glittering up in the woods. You backed up and said, "Hold on, is that a barrel?"

You sprinted up the hill and came back and said, "I left a barrel up there last harvest and totally forgot about it."

LUKE: Yeah, I remember how it all went down. The helicopter was buzzing the shit out of us. I was in a panic taking all this first cut and stuffing it into a garbage can. Then I lugged it around the hill away from the garden.

I was running around like a chicken with its head cut off — and then I would run off to some new project, ya know, trying to protect something else. Talk about your multitasking.

I had forgotten about that barrel until months later after the rains came. That's when I saw that little glint up there and thought, "Oh shit."

When I got there and poured it out, it was like split pea soup. What a shame because it was all first cut bud. But the ones that were right on top ... that had floated to the top, were actually salvageable.

POT SHORTS

Back then the demand was so great that if you could bag it, there was someone that wanted it. Any bud was acceptable as long as you could smoke it.

TOYOTA COMMERCIAL

LUKE: My red Toyota pickup could have starred in a Toyota commercial for all it went through one day. While working in our garden, with Toby driving my truck, we went to the house for something. He'd put the truck in gear but forgot to use the emergency brake on this steep hill. When he got out, it popped out of gear and started rolling. Here goes the truck, rolling down the hill past us with a full load of fertilizer in the back.

I ran to the door, but being on the steepest part of our property it was moving too fast. There was nothing we could do but just watch while it picked up speed — rolling at least two hundred yards — down through the meadow, past six or eight trees. Then we heard a crash.

"That's got to be totaled," I said, shaking my head.

"Yep," Toby replied.

When I got down there, I saw it had missed every tree except one branch, which smashed the windshield. It only stopped after it jumped a creek and plowed into a bank. The front bumper, winch, and hood were rolled back and crumpled but I managed to drive it out.

POT SHORTS

It didn't look like it could possibly run but, "Hey, it's a Toyota!" $4,600 dollars later it looked like new.

INCOGNITO

Incognito was one of the best gardeners who'd moved up from San Francisco. He was one of my first good friends who died of AIDS. Those were the days when we were first hearing about AIDS in the papers and some of our friends were getting sick. He grew some of the best pot on the mountain at that time. He was a fun, great guy.

LUKE: Incognito was growing down near Rock Creek and had three really successful years down there. I recall flying over with a pilot friend of ours, seeing how big the gardens were.

Incognito had stored all his weed in this little rock cave that was right down by the creek — a very cool and dry area. He would store it there for a month or so in cardboard boxes, which would equalize the moisture content in the weed.

That year there were these early rains that came. After three or four days of pouring rain, he was lying in bed enjoying the pleasant rumble of the creek below when it hit him: "My shit is under water!"

So he gets his flashlight and dashes out into the deluge and finds the whole cave submerged under boiling brown water. Hopping from boulder to boulder he goes downstream, and in the eddies he can see cardboard boxes and loose weed swirling around in

POT SHORTS

circles — a miserable sight, I'm sure. Most of it had already washed into the main river and was heading out to sea but he did manage to salvage a little bit of it. Funny, but upsetting, too.

It's A Mixed Bag

MAGOO

Magoo has curly brown hair, dreamy blue eyes, a crooked smile and plays a great banjo. He is extremely funny and keeps us all laughing.

Magoo got his nickname because of his thick glasses. Before corrective eye surgery, he couldn't see anything without them. Magoo and Luke loved to play pranks on each other.

LOLA: One summer, Luke planted a *huge* fake arrowhead on the path that Magoo walked on every day to check on his gardens. Luke rubbed dirt into it to make it look old, and then left it half uncovered. Over the weeks he kept going back and uncovering it more and more hoping Magoo would find it. Finally, Magoo's brother–in-law Red ended up finding it.

Red thought he'd hit the mother lode as it was probably the biggest arrowhead anyone had ever seen. He figured it had to be a ceremonial piece.

We heard through the grapevine that he had found it and was very excited and heading down to show it to a museum curator. The last thing Magoo saw as Red was heading down the hill in his truck was his arm outstretched with the arrowhead clenched in his fist, like a victory salute.

POT SHORTS

When Luke found out he quickly called him on the CB to tell him it was meant to be a prank on Magoo. Red didn't appreciate the humor, but was spared the embarrassment of showing it to someone for verification.

Had it been Magoo that found it, Luke would have never stopped him since they loved to play pranks on each other. And still do.

BITTEN BY THE BUG

LOLA: My crazy, adventurous girlfriend Sally had just received her pilot's license in Sonoma County and was eager to take off on a solo flight. She decided to fly up and surprise us by buzzing all around our house, hoping for us to come out and wave "Hi."

When we saw her a few weeks later, she expressed disappointment that we hadn't been there because she had wanted to throw a note out to us.

We had been home, but of course hadn't known it was her. All we saw was a plane circling overhead and inside the house we were totally freaking out, quite convinced that the pilot was reconnoitering our plants.

After the plane left we rushed to harvest our plants prematurely, once again bitten by the paranoia bug.

HAIR STRAIGHT UP

LUKE: I used to drive up to the mountain and bring these pot starts with me in my VW bus from the city. There were all these tall starts up above the windows. I had curtains, but you could kind of see through the curtains when the sun went through it.

And I'm driving through town and this cop was parked at a 90 degree angle watching traffic go by. So I thought I would just drive by him like everybody else is.

So I go by him and, BOOM, the red light goes on and he pulls up fast right behind me.

My hair went straight up, and I started to pull over and was thinking, "Christ on a crutch, I'm dead!" when he zooms around me and pulls over the car in front of me.

My heart was jumping out of my chest; I thought I was heading straight to jail.

It's A Mixed Bag

BEAN

LOLA: I think one of the most colorful characters that lived up here was Bean. He reminded me of Bobby Peru, a character in a David Lynch film. He looked the part, too, kind of scary, black greasy hair, piercing black eyes, just always watching you. He was suspicious of everyone, too.

Remember when that garden got ripped off down in your neck of the woods and a bunch of you found the tracks that led back to Chad and Shorty's place?

You guys went over there to confront him, and Bean happened to be painting for you guys so he went with you. Chad was sitting there at the table, giving you guys a mouth full of shit, blah, blah, blah.

CASSIE: Yeah, Chad had a gun on his table, and he started to reach for his gun, and you didn't see Bean hardly move. He was all of a sudden behind Chad with his little two-inch blade pocketknife next to Chad's throat. Bean had him in a headlock.

HANK: Yeah, Bean was just as calm as he could be.

Bean says to Chad, "Go ahead and pick up that pistol; you know you want to."

He acted as though it was not going to be any big deal to slit his throat, just like a chicken.

POT SHORTS

I'm thinking, "Man, is this going to be a bloodbath?"

We ended up leaving Chad that day with a warning.

HANK: Bean used to tell us these stories about how his dad told this guy one time, "Don't eat so much food or I'm going to kill ya."

He was apparently eating so much food, you know, he finally killed him. He finally shot him in the head.

He was just so matter of fact about telling that story.

CASSIE: I remember once, Bean telling me in his Southern redneck accent: "Some people are just like chickens, you know? You just want to cut their throats, just like a chicken."

HANK: His brothers were in prison, and I think his dad, too. He used to say his family would kill people if you paid them. You just have to come up with half the money up front and a picture of them, and they would collect the other half after they were killed.

He didn't like a lot of people — or orange cats either. According to Bean, orange cats only killed birds.

CASSIE: We would often give him a ride to town and he would like to just hang out and watch people cross the street, especially the ladies.

It's A Mixed Bag

HANK: He wasn't discriminatory with the ladies, though. He liked all shapes and sizes, especially ladies with big butts.

LUKE: He had leukemia for a long time before he died. Every time he felt real sick, he would head for the city and go on a major carrot juice cleanse. He would come back feeling revitalized and his color would be back.

LOLA: It's funny how you will make friends with people that you would normally have nothing to do with if you lived in town, but up in the hills it's important that you try to get along with all of your neighbors.

I'm glad he liked us because I wouldn't want to be on his hit list.

He was one of a kind though. My best memories of him are when he came over to paint. He would ride over on his ATV, get his comb out and slick back his hair; he'd have his cigarettes in his sleeve and that big grin, kind of like James Dean, but kind of creepy.

CASSIE: You'd say after he finished painting your house, "How much do I owe you, Bean?

He'd say, "How much you got in your pocket?"

I tell you what, I never thought I was going to miss him as much as I do.

HANK: Damn, could he paint.

POT SHORTS

MONEY WOES

LUKE: We were so busy during harvest. Lots of people up trimming, then you're stashing the trimmed bud and money outside for fear the law would come and bust you. You would just be so busy that you would forget where you hid your stuff.

Once I hid a paper bag with some money under the house intending to move it to a safer place later. I had this vindictive dog that would chew things up whenever I left her alone, but didn't think that bag would interest her.

I went to town to pick up a friend at the bus who was visiting for a few days, and when we drove down the driveway we could see this big mess of paper blowing all over the yard, with my dog standing there squirming happily.

When we got closer, we could see that it was all paper bills and the shredded bag that my dog had gotten hold of.

My friend said, "What the hell, look at all that money!"

I was very embarrassed but desperate to pick it up as fast as possible because the wind was still spreading it all over the place. My friend was laughing while we chased and gathered it.

It's A Mixed Bag

I didn't appreciate the humor, at least at the time, but was glad for the help.

......

LUKE: Another time my friend Julie couldn't find a large stash of money she had buried. For two or three years she returned to where she thought it was buried and kept digging more holes in her search. Soon the whole hillside looked like pigs had rooted it. Finally, I got another friend with an excavator to rip up the whole area until the money finally popped up.

Julie was a happy gal since she had pretty much given up on finding the money and she really needed it.

......

GOLDIE: I remember getting the coins out of piggy banks to go do laundry. I thought I hardly had a penny to my name because we were just barely making the bills. But, doggone it, the next year when Gator was ready to put some pot away, he found a little stack of bills.

I said, "We really could have used that."

......

TOBY: Once I found a jar I must have stashed in a pile of bricks. A good hiding place, I guess. I opened it

POT SHORTS

up and there was just one solid chunk of old moldy bills stuck together — which had once been a good amount.

Another time my safe filled up with water and was all rusted out. Since we were leaving town the next day, we stayed up all night long trying to dry out this soggy, snotty money.

So I told the bank it was my father's money that he'd buried somewhere. I've still got some. It's legal money, but the numbers must be readable on one side and you have to find the right bank to exchange it.

LUKE: So that's a good lesson: No matter how bad the money looks, you can still redeem it.

I found some money that I put in the back of my truck and it got wet and became a cake of money that I couldn't separate.

I gave it to the bank and they sent it to wherever they send it, and the amount that came back was more than I even anticipated. They knew *exactly* how much was there.

CASSIE: The heavy equipment operator always would smell the money you'd give him. I asked him why and he said, "Because so much of the money smells like pot and I just don't like taking that money."

Some people actually launder the money that smells like pot. They really do run it through the washing machine.

GOLDIE: We did. And we threw it in the dryer with a whole bunch of Downy sheets. It came out smelling sweet — so fluffy and nice.

It's A Mixed Bag

Friends came over and we said, "Hey, you want to see how we launder our money?"

And we opened the dryer door.

......

CASSIE: I've got a good laundry story.

A friend, who was worried about someone breaking into her house, kept pot in her safe along with her money. When she returned some money she owed me, I noticed it smelled strongly of pot. What was I to do?

I had bought a bunch of onion bagels, so I shoved the money down in the onion bagels, hoping that would help because I needed to make a deposit at the bank.

Well, I walked into the bank and there was a bake sale going on there. While I waited in line, trying to be nonchalant with my cash deposit now smelling like pot *and* onion bagels, I was trying to act cool. I'm watching and trying to figure out what this bake sale is all about.

And then I see this giant banner and a woman who worked at the bank was yelling, "Help raise money for our children. Just say no to drugs!"

It was absolutely crazy. And all these people were going, "Oh, yeah!" while the loud-mouthed lady gave out cookies.

All I could think was, "Oh, my God. I'll never do this again."

......

LUKE: Carrying cash instead of credit cards can lead to bad things, too.

One time we were traveling in Mexico and riding in a first class bus and I was carrying all of our money. It was a lot of money as we were traveling for a good long while. It was in a black money belt strapped around my waist.

When I went to the toilet in the rear of the bus, I unsnapped the elastic belt and it whipped around my body and flew straight down the toilet hole. A rush of panic went through me while I imagined it down there out of reach floating in that brown soup.

I couldn't see down because there wasn't enough light. Options are running through my head. Do I tell the driver and offer him a reward to get it? Do I see if I can reach it?

I decide to pull up my sleeves and reach deep. I can just barely touch something with my fingertip that feels like my belt, but it's not moving around like it would be in a soup.

So now I'm thinking it's probably my belt balancing on top of a brown cone shape of shit and if I knock it off its back to square one.

It's A Mixed Bag

I stretch all the way with my ear stuck to the seat and manage to use my fingers like a pair of tweezers and pinch it with the tips.

Up and out it came, black, brown, and beautiful.

After a thorough cleaning I came out and told my friends what had happened, and had to put up with their good humored "ooooh, don't touch me, " for the rest of the day.

life on the mountain

POT SHORTS

THE DAY PACK

CASSIE: I think our kids got a really good start by being taught to love learning and I really credit the teachers and the parents who were involved in the school. Even the kids who are going to the school right now are exceptional in that they have big dreams and love to learn. My son Zack knew he could compete at the university level, even though he was coming from a little rural school in a tiny podunk place. He probably had more support by a family of adults than if we lived somewhere like Santa Rosa.

Zack was always a straight A student — well-rounded, conscientious and mature. He can really talk to people and is quite aware of how people are making a living here. Right now he's very committed to becoming an engineer. He graduated from a class of four students and went on to Southern California University where he's doing great.

It was always important to us that we never lied to Zack about what we did. We basically started out telling him that pot is an herb that is used for people who were sick, or people who needed to sleep, things like that. As he got older, we let him know that it was against the law. Some things are against the law and shouldn't be. That is where we kind of left it. But he always knew it and we never had a problem.

POT SHORTS

We made it okay for him to talk with family and we picked about four people in the family that he could go to and talk about anything at all — about the pot or about us as parents, anything. He was just asked to keep it in the family.

Later on, he told me that most of the kids in school had parents who were in some way involved in the business. As a teenager, he revealed that even some teachers were growing pot. He knew that because their children were his classmates. As they got older, they shared information with each other when they felt safe.

Some of the kids that Zack went to school with had righteous attitudes about pot. It was basically because their parents had lied to them and told them that they had legal businesses, minimizing the pot growing aspect. And these kids developed attitudes against pot growers. Some of these parents may still be lying to their children and I don't think that's a healthy family dynamic.

What ended up being a real positive thing for us was our involvement with the school. Because we got to know the kids and their parents, whenever Zack went home with a friend we already knew the parents. Everybody lived forty-five minutes from school — a long distance when you think about it.

When Zack was probably thirteen or fourteen, junior high school age, I got a phone call one day at lunchtime.

"Mom, what the hell?" Zack said. "There's a black backpack here and it's got pot in it. It's not my pot, Mom. It must belong to one of your friends ... one of your stoned out friends!"

And it was totally Lizzy's pot — a good friend of mine who is always smoking pot. It turns out she ended up sticking her entire stash in the black backpack which she thought belonged to her, but it really belonged to Zack.

He was like, "What the hell? If I get in trouble for this .... I don't know what to do with it. What do I do with it Mom?"

I'm like, "Just keep your cool, Zack. It's fine. Bring it back home, and everything will be OK."

Zack is ultra conservative and this mix up really freaked him out.

Another thing that has been hard for him and many of the kids who went on to college is to watch their classmates who remain here growing pot and making tons of money. It's difficult for them to work so hard trying to land a job in their chosen profession only to realize that their classmates here on the mountain are making all kinds of money, sometimes right out of high school.

When Zack comes home from college it's hard for him to see that so and so has a giant 4 x 4 truck and he's got this and he's got that and he gets to go snowboarding all winter and doesn't have to go to school and try to land a job. In my opinion, however, that guy does have to work hard — at growing pot.

POT SHORTS

For most of the kids who've gone away to college, their parents have explained, "This pot thing isn't going to last forever. Once there is no longer a market for growing illegal pot, you'll need to go to college to get a job."

WANTING BABIES

CASSIE: My friend Winkers and I decided we both wanted to have babies, but it wasn't going to happen for free. My husband and I were living on a shoestring, as were they. The money from our home gardens was off limits because that was needed for living expenses. So we came up with a plan to put in a "baby garden."

She and I decided we could do this. We already grew enough pot to make a living, so we would split whatever money we made from the baby garden to investigate fertility work and our options for getting pregnant. We named the baby garden "Joe." We made a pact as to how we were going to pull it off and we would ask each other, "Did you check on Joe?"

We hiked way uphill to Dog Creek, about one and a half miles. It's very steep land, lots of boulders and water. We brought in five gallon buckets and we scraped the topsoil from under the oaks. The most difficult thing to carry in was the large storage bladder which served as our water tank. But we packed it in and put it up in the trees.

Winkers had an idea as to where the property line was between these two absentee property owners, so we decided we'd get the water from one side and grow the pot on the other side. If one or the other property owners finds this garden way the hell up there, they'll think it belongs to the other guy, and won't even suspect it's two women up there growing pot.

Winkers thought the starts we were packing in would survive just fine. We shook the dirt out of them and lay them in a box — just the bare roots. The plan was to carry them in and plant them that same day. The only way we could get water was out of the creek. We would pack in one charged car battery (for pumping) and take out the discharged one on our backs the same day. We did this for years.

Winkers did a whole fertility thing, a lot of costly stuff, but I got my baby and sadly she didn't. And when my son was only a teeny baby I decided there was no way in hell that I was going to keep growing there, because I didn't sleep at night and then I would have to get up at 6:00 a.m.

We would go in before CAMP came, and then get out. If CAMP came, one of us would have to run up there and drag all those potted plants back into hiding. We'd wait until the heli was gone, then return in the afternoon and drag them all back into the sun.

They were the piddliest little plants, but we were able to do our whole fertility thing with the money.

We got very good at rock hopping and I got to the point where I could move up that creek, running in and out, with a battery on my back.

Life On The Mountain

GROWING UP ON THE MOUNTAIN

We were having a birthday gathering at a neighbor's pond. Some of the kids (now young adults) grew up there, went off to college, and returned to live and have families of their own. There were also a couple of young women just visiting, but who had also grown up there. I decided to ask them how living up in the pot community might have affected them.

SHORTCAKE: I moved up to the mountain when I was two years old in 1984. I eventually went to school in a one-room schoolhouse with only four other kids in the school. At that point, only a select group of people had landlines; most used CB radios to communicate. There happened to be a very flat spot on a property that was next to the school. The helicopters and the vehicle convoys would gather on that flat spot before going back to try to bust all the neighbors. I remember all the kids lining up to use the phone to call our emergency numbers to the few people that had landlines. We had a huge phone tree and they would get on the CB radios and warn all the neighbors that CAMP was on the hill.

For as long as I can remember, it was normal. We never grew on our own property, property that had our name on it, so we always felt safe. Most of the people that had children did not grow on their own properties. They might own other properties that they grew on, but it would be in a friend's name, or someone would give them a percentage for growing pot for them.

SUSIE: I never thought it was bad, I never thought it was something to be ashamed of. Part of that had to do with how it was dealt with. It was never hidden from me or treated as something to be ashamed of. I always pretty much understood that there were some places that you couldn't talk about it, but I also remember how it affects your life as a kid growing up. I had lots of birthday parties that were dampened by helicopters flying around. My dad had to leave various birthday parties because CAMP was flying.

I've never lived with any other family and every family must have stress, and ours had certain levels of stress at certain times of year. There's nowhere near as much now but when I was a kid, the helicopters flying, the rip-offs, caravans coming up the hill, it created a certain level of stress. I think also, being raised in a situation like that makes you kind of permanently and naturally suspicious of any sort of law enforcement.

I also have great memories of everyone celebrating the different holidays together and everyone on the mountain would come. I remember it being a good feeling. Everybody seemed happy and appreciated being around each other. It was a pretty peaceful feeling. Nobody seemed shady.

I think it's harder for some people, you know, families that happen to grow weed in town, and all of their friends' parents have regular jobs. I never experienced that. All of my friends' parents on the mountain grew. What makes you feel bad is when you feel like an outsider and I don't think most of us felt that way.

I remember a funny story. We were in town buying groceries. I had remembered seeing tortillas in a bag of pot before, to hydrate it. When you're a little kid you like to show your parents how well you pay attention to things, and I remember thinking, "I'll show him how much I pay attention."

So I'm standing at the counter and I say, "Are you buying those tortillas to put in your bag of pot, Daddy?"

I remember the lady looking at me — and my dad said, "No, I'm not."

Then when we got outside to the car, he explained to me — very clearly, not in a weird way— that, "Not everyone knows what we do, and it's nothing to feel bad about, but we just don't talk about it."

It was the only conversation like that we ever had. I just thought "Oh, okay, we just don't talk about it."

I don't remember feeling weird. Well actually, when the lady looked at me I remember feeling a little weird.

MATILDA: I remember being scared a lot, scared that my mom was going to get in trouble. But I also think there were a lot of positive things about it, too, because my mom got to stay home with me all the time. I didn't have to go to daycare from 8:00 in the morning to 6:30 anymore once we moved up on the hill. I feel like that was really special.

But I do remember being scared a lot and I still kind of freak out a little bit. My mom was never secretive about it so I had a hard time being secretive about it. I felt like that would mean I was doing something wrong or bad.

I feel like we are farmers, and the pharmaceutical companies, the tobacco and alcohol companies are much worse.

We're open with our kids about it as well. I don't feel growing pot is wrong. It's so open now; nobody even tries to hide it anymore.

It's so drastically different, there's not even a comparison. I know people now who are surprised how it's changed since the mid '80s to late '90s. There was a lot more money to eradicate pot in those days. There was more effort, and it was way more of an underground thing.

Now nobody tries to hide it at all. There are people in town with plants in trucks. I've seen people with scissors taped to their "need work" signs on the side of the road.

The first time people were growing full-sized plants outside in full sun, everybody thought they were crazy, but now everybody's doing it.

I remember driving down the road, past the CAMP trucks and you'd see the plants hanging out of the truck. COG (Citizens Observation Group) members

Life On The Mountain

were following them around, taking pictures of them. They were going to right all the wrongs.

I think it's special that I get to be with my kids most of the time. I work really hard but I can schedule my own time. I can volunteer to work at their school, with soccer, and be on the school board. If I had a 9 to 5 job I wouldn't be able to do any of that stuff. There's a lot that I feel really fortunate about.

I remember talking to my neighbor down below about the old days. Then, every time a helicopter went over she was shaking and freaking out. Now, she goes into the local gas station and there were "roaches" on the floor. People smoke a joint out in the parking lot and put out the roach when they walk in the door. People are just so open everywhere. People talk about it so freely, too.

We had to talk with our daughter because — and this is a great example of how much kids are paying attention — my husband came out of the woods with a barrel and a bag, and she was like, "Look at you, Dad. You're so crazy, with a barrel of money and a bag of weed."

And I was like, "Oh shit, really?"

I think she was a kindergartener then and he came home and told me, "I guess we have to have the talk now."

My daughter said to me in the car the other day, "Well, I know what you do, Mom."

I said, "What do you mean? You know what I do besides drive you around?"

POT SHORTS

"Because you take care of us and you trim," she said.

This is a conversation that all these little kids at school are having together. So we had the conversation about talking about this with really close family and friends but you don't talk to just any people about it.

But everybody's doing it. I would be surprised if most of the people in town don't grow. Most everybody now is connected in some way or other. They are at least trimming part time or know someone that is.

PESTO: As a kid, I wasn't allowed to talk to anyone except my best friend about it. That's because her parents did the same thing. We'd share the experience of picking little pieces of pot out of our socks.

And if anybody asked what the green stuff was, we'd say "It's grass from hiking in the woods."

We both became accustomed to playing along with the story of what our parents did for a living. When one of our dads had to sleep out in the garden to guard from the rip-offs, we'd sleep at each other's house. We grew up not trusting cops and hating helicopters.

Anyway, over the years, growing pot became more legal and a lot more prevalent. Everyone we knew was doing it and, locally, most people just assumed you did it if you lived up on the hill. You almost became desensitized to the illegality of it all ... until you brought an outsider in. It seems to be a lot safer now, in comparison to how it used to be, but it's still a risk.

Life On The Mountain

JOSIE: I remember my friend Pesto and I being at a party when we were little and meeting another little girl who was bragging that she knew what "weed" was because her parents grew it.

Pesto and I didn't say anything but we were thinking, "Why is she telling us this?"

We knew from a young age, it just wasn't something we talked about, especially to strangers.

I always knew my parents grew pot, but I don't think I ever really thought much about it. I loved living in the most beautiful place I could think of and in the wonderful community I grew up in, but I never really thought about the fact that growing pot was what made this possible or that the life we had up there was unique to the business my parents were in. I just loved being a country girl. I remember being called a "city girl" once when I was young, and I think it may have been the most insulted I'd ever felt.

Once I got older I began trimming. I'd go up the hill to work for the weekend and then back down to college for the week.

Working with pot creates a bit of a problem for me in that when I meet someone new, one of the first questions he or she often asks is, "What do you do for work?" or "How do you make money?"

I try to stay on other topics like hobbies, side jobs or interests; it always makes me feel bad when I can't be fully honest or when people think I don't do much in the way of work, especially in the Fall when I'm working a lot.

Nonetheless, I love the work, I feel lucky to have met so many wonderful people over the years, and to have the freedom it allows. Really, it's worth feeling a little uncomfortable sometimes.

GATHERING OF THE HILL FOLK

LILY: Because we live so rurally up here — most of us easily an hour from the closest podunk little town — our socialization came about quite naturally. We had wonderful gatherings, which were a really nice way to get to know your neighbors. We became aware of each other, even though each of us had at least twenty acres and we couldn't see each other's homes.

We created a sense of community— that feeling in life that when the village is missing, we will create one.

You can live in a neighborhood where a house is right next to you but you don't know your neighbors. We were blessed in really knowing who our neighbors were. The sense of security we had wasn't because we were all the same kind of people. We were from all different walks of life but we bonded because of our ruralness and our lifestyle. We bonded in the sense of one hand helping another, being very in tune with each other's need for help or work or falling upon hard times when the crop didn't come in.

We all pulled together and helped each other get through the year, much like the old days with barn raisings and community potlucks. We actually did have a house-raising for someone who needed a home for

POT SHORTS

their son, daughter-in-law and new baby. We got together for a weekend and put up a little house.

To this day we still gather, not quite as often as we used to when we were much younger, but we still gather.

By now we've known many of our neighbors for more than thirty-five years — something that's really missing in our society. Being able to get along, even with each other's differences, accepting the differences and understanding the strengths — now these are qualities we have come to value. We have second and third generation people living here now, and some of the kids that we carpooled to school now have their own children and are doing their own carpooling.

My parents lived here. Our child who came of age here now lives here with her children. And that is very common in these hills. I think it speaks to the viability of the land, the viability of how we make our living, and how that community security is celebrated in this day and time of the faceless masses.

HOLIDAYS

LOLA: We were a very tight-knit group and would get together for any little excuse. Our play dates with the children would be lunches, hikes, painting, and sometimes swimming at whichever pond was nearby. Sunday afternoons we met for volleyball games on our property.

Birthday parties ... well, the whole mountain would be invited when it was a child's birthday. All the children would put on their fancy clothes and we would have several birthday cakes, games and a piñata. For Easter, we had our annual Easter egg and scavenger hunt for the children, followed by one for the adults in which everyone would throw five dollars into a huge plastic egg, and someone would win a cash prize.

All of these events, of course, included delicious potlucks which gave everyone an opportunity to show off their culinary skills. If it was cold or snowing, which happened sometimes during Easter, we would just bundle up and go on with the party.

But the best event of the year was Halloween. Dale and his boyfriend Gunther would actually build a stage in their living room. They always did an incredible job adorning the place with chandeliers hanging from the ceiling and decorations matching each year's theme. We would basically put on a variety show involving all the kids and adults and guests who wanted to take part. We made costumes and practiced for months, usually

POT SHORTS

choreographing different dance routines and lip-syncing to old tunes. One year, the theme was Marilyn Monroe and everybody dressed as Marilyn, Marilyn's mother, Marilyn back from the dead, Joe DiMaggio, or President Kennedy. Another time, the theme was *Hair Spray*. Then came *Saturday Night Fever* in which, of course, we did disco numbers and dressed accordingly. People would do dances and skits from musicals or any combination of the above. Kids did everything from *The Nutcracker* to lip-syncing to Leslie Gore.

I remember one year, filming the cute kids on stage all doing the Macarena when the theme was *Rocky Horror Picture Show*. Scanning the crowd, I saw many of our men friends being good sports, dressed in full-body lingerie and heels and dancing the Macarena along with the kids.

Now, every time I watch that video, I feel so happy that all our kids grew up in such an open-minded and loving environment. Whoever was performing, the audience was always hooting and hollering — the most supportive audience you could ever ask for, and these parties continued for ten years.

That era ended on New Year's Eve in the year 2000 with a huge bonfire at Cooper's and dancing into the wee hours. The next morning we all met at Cassie's for a big breakfast. We placed everything from locks of hair, to fingernails and pot, to notes, into a time capsule, then we took a hike and buried it deep in this rocky area down by the creek. After that, we went up to our house and ate pozole (a Latin inspired stew) while we watched the last ten years of Halloween party videos.

Life On The Mountain

......

Over a decade has passed now and we still gather and get involved in our costumes but it's not quite the same. At a recent party, we each came dressed as a strain of pot. I was dressed as "Train Wreck," and Luke was "Monkey Balls." Others were everything from "Sweet Tooth" to "Blue Dog," "Killer Blue," "Royal Kush," "Purple Urkle," "Silver," and many more.

There was even someone dressed as white powdery mildew. The guy was completely white and covered in talcum powder, walking around shaking on everyone.

Another party in early October stemmed from donations that had been made from some of the people in the community to go into Goldie and Gator's special garden. They had asked people if they would donate a plant in their favorite strain that they had developed themselves.

Everyone came and took photos of these beautiful plants — made especially beautiful by the knowledge that the plant proceeds were going to their favorite charities.

last but not least

POT SHORTS

Last But Not Least

HIGH FLYERS' CLUB

Marijuana has made a long journey over the years. The days of growing two-ounce, poor quality, shade plants and smoking in secret are being replaced with large, sun-drenched beauties from top genetics, smoked openly at nice social gatherings.

Zoey Smith lives atop a ridge in Sonoma County wine country with her attorney husband, their blind Abyssinian cat and 3 goats. She retired as a San Francisco interior designer and now devotes time to environmental and political campaigns.

She was telling me about a group she recently joined called The High Flyers' Club. *This mix of baby boomers consists of individuals from the wine industry, conservationists, and retirees. Most of them have experienced pot over the years, but not particularly in any kind of gourmet way.*

Zoey: It is a laughing and learning experience simultaneously. Each month, there is a host responsible for procuring a different strain of pot to hand out to each of our members. Agendas are passed around the table with evaluation sheets. The previous month's samples had been taken home, savored and critiqued. Experiences are then shared and compared.

Admittedly, our meetings soon drift from the agenda. It is pretty hilarious, really. Mocking more

POT SHORTS

serious Board meetings we've all been a part of, our Chair will call us back to order.

It's trippy to tailor our Cannabis evaluations using a similar approach as wine: color, nose, and taste. Just as generic jug wine gave way to specific terroir and quality varietals, so early weed has evolved to many high quality tasty strains.

A notable difference in ratings is that wine judges ignore the "high" that wine brings. With grass, the way you feel varies with the strain and the percentage of Sativa or Indica. We love Sativa for its lighter, creative side, boosting the imagination and energy. Indica is just what the doctor ordered for feeling a full body relaxation.

The agenda includes an opportunity to bring new paraphernalia to show the group. For instance vaporizers. Vaporizers are easier on the lungs since you breathe in lovely vapors, the essence, not the harsh smoke. If you are going to indulge, why not make it the best? Now I even keep my pot organized in antique Moroccan containers, whereas it used to be in a shoebox.

For me, grass opens a portal to tap deeper into senses, realizing an even fuller potential to enhance what I see, hear, taste and (my personal favorite) touch. Alcohol? Not always where I want to be.

Last But Not Least

I don't know about you, but I'm sniffing change in the air. Or is that skunk?

POT SHORTS

THIS LAND IS YOUR LAND, THIS LAND IS MY LAND

ZOEY: There is No Planet "B."

The back-to-the-land people in Lola and Luke's community shared a great appreciation for the natural environment. In fact, smoking marijuana actually enhanced that appreciation. Surely, it was one of the catalysts to "Earth Day" and the Green movement. They tended their gardens growing organically with TLC sometimes even giving them names.

But now irony hits hard. The earthmovers and chainsaws have been cutting across the landscape bringing a black cloud over the forests, streams and wildlife.

Historically, natural resource commodities in the West, have taken a toll on the environment. Gold extraction used hydraulic mega-hoses destroying hillsides leaving tailings of lost hope damming the streams with little regulation. Redwood trees were next ... thousand-year-old heritage giants falling right and left, unsustainably. Then agricultural efforts became aggressive, using pesticides and herbicides depleting soil and water life, growing mono crops of grapes for wine. The new gold rush is for growing marijuana. It is now in a lawless unregulated zone, getting bigger and more dangerous every day.

Last But Not Least

As the *NY Times* reports, Google Earth reveals huge swaths of forests clear-cut to plant the once almost-sacred weed. Wildlife habitat is squeezed and salmon streams are diminished with toxic runoff. The new breed of mega-grower is not from the rootstock of the original people. They see a product, not a community. They see gold. They see no regulations.

LOLA: *We need to legalize in order to be able to regulate, and THE SOONER THE BETTER. Take the inflated profit away from the growers and use a fraction of the money on prosecution and incarceration to educate and treat the hardcore drug addiction, and everyone would benefit. The senseless "War on Drugs" has created a monster in the form of cartels from here to south of the border. When we finally wake up and end this crazy war, they will be forced to move on and our world will be a better place.*

ACKNOWLEDGMENTS

I feel tremendous gratitude to the people who have shared their stories. Without them this book would never have been possible. Many friends and family read the manuscript at various stages, and I am indebted to them all, especially Rubia and Kelly for encouraging me when I needed it the most.

A special thanks to CJ for modeling for the front cover and for doing the artwork for this book. I'm grateful to Elysa for taking time to come to the mountain and take photographs for the cover and for helping so much. Quick Bird, you rock with your amazing computer skills.

A special thanks to Shonnie for her highly valued encouragement and suggestions that have added so much to this book. Annabel, thanks for your editing contributions.

Thank you, Zoey, for all of your work transcribing, editing, and helping with decisions. You were constantly there as my wing-woman believing in the telling of these stories. Without you I don't think I would have had the courage to pursue this.

Sue, my lifelong friend who stepped in and made this all come to fruition, I love you with all my heart.

Last but not least, to my adorable husband, Luke. He not only contributed stories and helped me edit but was my rock throughout the process. In looking back over our life on the hill and all the experiences that brought...the hard work, the anxiety and stress, the laughter and the love, there is no one I would rather have gone through all of this with than him. I have watched him grow into the best husband, father and man I have ever known.

— Lola Larkin